You're Not the Boss of Me

TOMICA ATKINSON

You're Not the Boss of Me

ARCHWAY PUBLISHING

Copyright © 2017 Tomica Atkinson.

All rights reserved. No part of this book may be used or reproduced by any means, graphic, electronic, or mechanical, including photocopying, recording, taping or by any information storage retrieval system without the written permission of the author except in the case of brief quotations embodied in critical articles and reviews.

Archway Publishing books may be ordered through booksellers or by contacting:

Archway Publishing
1663 Liberty Drive
Bloomington, IN 47403
www.archwaypublishing.com
1 (888) 242-5904

Because of the dynamic nature of the Internet, any web addresses or links contained in this book may have changed since publication and may no longer be valid. The views expressed in this work are solely those of the author and do not necessarily reflect the views of the publisher, and the publisher hereby disclaims any responsibility for them.

Any people depicted in stock imagery provided by Thinkstock are models, and such images are being used for illustrative purposes only. Certain stock imagery © Thinkstock.

Scripture taken from the King James Version of the Bible.

Scripture quotations marked (NIV) are taken from the Holy Bible, New International Version®, NIV®. Copyright © 1973, 1978, 1984, 2011 by Biblica, Inc.™ Used by permission of Zondervan. All rights reserved worldwide. www.zondervan.com The "NIV" and "New International Version" are trademarks registered in the United States Patent and Trademark Office by Biblica, Inc.™

This book is a work of non-fiction. Unless otherwise noted, the author and the publisher make no explicit guarantees as to the accuracy of the information contained in this book and in some cases, names of people and places have been altered to protect their privacy.

ISBN: 978-1-4808-5394-2 (sc)
ISBN: 978-1-4808-5393-5 (hc)
ISBN: 978-1-4808-5395-9 (e)

Library of Congress Control Number: 2017917813

Print information available on the last page.

Archway Publishing rev. date: 12/4/2017

CONTENTS

Acknowledgments vii
Introduction ix
Section I   In the Midst of a Storm 1
    Strategy 1: Brainstorming
Chapter 1   Lost in Life 3
Chapter 2   Getting Back on the Right Path 15
Chapter 3   Calming the Storm 19
Section II   Rainy Days 23
    Strategy 2: Researching
    Strategy 3: Planning
    Strategy 4: Implementing
Chapter 4   Asking For Directions 25
Chapter 5   Quick Systems Check— Preparing for Your
    Journey 42
Chapter 6   Getting in the Driver's Seat 47
Chapter 7   Ready, Set, Go! 79
Section III   Sunny Days 85
    Strategy 5: Evaluating
    Strategy 6: Living
Chapter 8   Route Check 87
Chapter 9   You Have Arrived at Your Destination 92
Business Lessons 97

ACKNOWLEDGMENTS

First, I want to thank my heavenly father. Without my spiritual growth, none of this would have been possible. My faith has grown tremendously, allowing me to overcome my fears; walk by faith and not by sight; and take leap after leap towards my dreams.

Thanks to all my family, friends, business partners, and associates for your love and support. Thanks for listening and for your encouraging words, and sometimes for being my test subjects for my books and other business ventures. Words can't express how much I appreciate all the unconditional love and support of my mom; dads; grandparents; siblings; uncles; aunts; cousins; and in-laws. Even when we didn't agree on everything, your actions spoke your love loud and clear. Thank you for helping me become the woman I am today. Thank you, Grandma Doll and Uncle Wesley; may you both continue to rest in heaven. Thanks to everyone who has made an impact on my family and my life. I wish I could list everyone individually, but this book would be way too long.

I even want to thank the ones who weren't supportive, because the negativity motivated me even more. I feed off negativity; it is just a confirmation from God that I am on the right path. No one is going to come at you if you aren't doing anything worthwhile or if they don't feel intimidated by you. Thanks for helping bring out in me what I needed to be my own boss.

I've saved the best for last. I especially want to thank my husband

and our sons. You all have always been my motivation for everything I do in life. Thank you for listening to all my ideas. Thank you for believing in me. Thank you for allowing me to take the time away from our family life to write and build businesses. Thank you for trusting that I would put my laptop down whenever you needed me. I am a woman of God, a wife, and a mother first and foremost. You all know that nothing would take priority over my guys. Thank you for sharing me with the world! I will always and forever love you unconditionally.

INTRODUCTION

Just sitting thinking …

I don't want to work anymore. I am so tired of working for someone else. There are so many other things I want to do instead of sitting in a cubicle all day, frustrated. I refuse to hit a time clock for the rest of my life, living paycheck to paycheck. There's more to life than this. Others may be okay with that, but I'm not.

I know people aren't okay with this. I've heard my friends, family, and coworkers talk about this almost every day. The constant complaining about their work schedule, job duties, coworkers, supervisor, salary, work environment—the list goes on and on. We all feel overworked, unappreciated, and underpaid in our jobs. Where is the loyalty and the concern for employee morale? Why are some put in management positions to supervise and lead employees when they do not have any leadership skills? Why are so many undeserving people getting promotions? I'm doing all the right things and still being overlooked.

When you throw in everything else going on in my personal life with family, finances, health, and personal wellness, this is just way too much to deal with. Something is very wrong with this picture. I know a lot of people who are actively seeking and interviewing for other employment but just haven't gotten an offer yet. On the other hand, I know quite a few entrepreneurs. I have always wanted to start my own business. I should be my own boss. Well, what's stopping me? Maybe fear. What if I fail at what I want to do?

What has the world we live in evolved into? The rich get richer, the middle class stays broke, and the poor get poorer. Seems to be a tremendous gap in the mind-set, education, and motivation of the three classes of individuals. We must do something to bridge the gaps. It's ridiculous to live in a world in which we allow this to be our norm.

We need to educate our communities and create opportunities for individuals to be self-sufficient. It's possible. Black Wall Street existed, so there is no doubt in my mind. My God, every time I think about how it was all destroyed in the blink of an eye, I get furious. Despite my emotions, the point is it existed. Why can't we get that back?

I can only imagine the world we could be living in if we bridged those gaps. Seeing communities thriving, filled with different levels of prosperous and self-sufficient individuals—not from a handout, but from an opportunity. Not from any type of government program, but from the fruits of their own vision, knowledge, power, and labor. I know the Bible says in Proverbs 29:18 (KJV) "Where there is no vision the people perish." Because there is no vision, these gaps continue to grow wider and wider.

This world is set up for us to fail. Why are we only teaching our children to get a college education to create thousands of dollars of debt and put limits on their lives by telling them to go get a job, work for thirty years, and retire? It is so funny how we go to work and the manager tells us what to do all day long. We give 110 percent to a job without any hesitation for someone else, but we won't do it for ourselves. I realize we were programmed to be that way; it won't end until we break the cycle.

So, what am I going to do? I am going to use all of my hurt and *frustration as motivation to change myself and to inspire others to change too. I am going to break that cycle. I will be my own boss. You are not the boss of me. I am my own boss.*

These are just my thoughts. But these conclusions come from more than my own opinion. In my research, I found that 30 percent of the 150,000 full- and part-time workers surveyed honestly enjoyed their jobs and their bosses—and that is where the good news stops. The other 70 percent of Americans surveyed in the 2013 Gallup poll either hated their jobs or were completely disengaged, and not even incentives and extras could relieve them from the workingman's blues. Of that 70 percent, a full 20 percent are what Gallup classifies as "actively disengaged." These are the people who quietly voice their frustrations and complaints to their coworkers and job hunt on their lunch breaks. The remaining 50 percent of US workers are labeled as "disengaged," according to the report. While they show up for work, they are not "inspired by their managers." Many of those surveyed complained of "bosses from hell" who ignored talent and didn't cultivate growth.

But the implications of the report go much deeper. The report stated that the dissatisfaction, anger, and boredom felt by workers hurts the economy, which has been feeble since the Great Recession of 2008. It costs the US an estimated $450 billion to $550 billion per annum of lost productivity, stolen goods, and missed days of work.[1] How's that for honesty?

Again, I ask, why does it have to be like this? Who can you blame for feeling like this? What do you do in this situation when you just feel stuck and all hope is lost? Enough is enough—no more complaining. It is time to do something about the frustration.

---

[1] Victor Lipman, "Surprising, Disturbing Facts from the Mother of All Employee Engagement Surveys," *Forbes*, September 23, 2013, https://www.forbes.com/sites/victorlipman/2013/09/23/surprising-disturbing-facts-from-the-mother-of-all-employee-engagement-surveys/#45f832273120.

The simple answer to all your questions is, you cannot control the actions of anyone else; you can only control your own actions and remove yourself from a bad situation. It is time to realize that you are already your own boss. You control everything—the good, the bad, and the ugly. It's all you! Some other individuals and situations may influence you along the way, but it is your decision to be a leader or a follower; to pay your bills on time or go shopping; to open a new credit card to get 25 percent off your purchase today or not because you already have $10,000 worth of credit-card debt; to stay in or leave that toxic relationship; or to stay on that job for thirty years when you are miserable or start your own business.

Are you starting to get my point? I hope so, because the choices here are yours. It can be hard to see that when you have so much going on around you, I know. You feel like you are in a storm while traveling through this journey called life.

In this book, you will find a road map based on my six simple strategies to empower you to transition from full-time employee to full-time entrepreneur, or to your dream career whatever it may be. You will quickly discover that this book is not only about becoming an entrepreneur but also about creating strategies and implementing them. You will discover that the true meaning of being your own boss starts with changing your mind-set and realizing that you must create the opportunities to live the life you desire.

Regardless of whether you desire to be a business owner or climb the corporate ladder to your dream job—or maybe you still haven't quite figured it out yet—you still must be your own boss to get to that destination. It is a mind-set you essentially acquire, and this book will guide you every step of the way. Obviously, you are ready for a change, because you are reading this book. Now, let's take this journey together. It won't be easy, but with this roadmap to guide you through the storm, you will reach those sunny days of your paradise destination living the life you've always dreamed of.

Before we get started, I just want to thank you for purchasing book 1 of the "I Am My Own Boss' Mind-set" book series. Stay tuned for book 2.

IN THE MIDST OF A STORM

Strategy 1: Brainstorming

CHAPTER 1
LOST IN LIFE

Stop for a second. Get in a quiet place and just stop for a second. We get so caught up in everything around us that we don't recognize that we are lost. We lose our sense of direction. We continue to travel down that same road of frustration, disappointment, broken relationships, unfulfilled dreams, and debt. We think we have it all together, but we really don't.

You may be doing well in one area of your life but not well in other areas. Do you realize that these things are connected? Prolonged stress over your career will affect your personal health and well-being, your finances, and your family life. According to the American Psychological Association, prolonged stress can affect all of your organs—including both male and female reproductive systems—and create stress-related disorders like tension and migraine headaches; asthma; panic attacks; hypertension; heart attack; stroke; diabetes; heartburn or acid reflux; ulcers; and diarrhea or constipation. Stress can affect testosterone production and sperm production, and it can cause erectile dysfunction in men. For women, stress can cause irregular menstrual cycles, make premenstrual symptoms worse, and reduce sexual drive.[2]

---
[2] "Understanding Chronic Stress," American Psychological Association, accessed July 12, 2017, http://www.apa.org/helpcenter/understanding-chronic-stress.aspx.

All that seems like a high price to pay for staying in a job you're unhappy with. I don't know about you, but I wouldn't continue to risk my health. Are you going to be the person who ignores all the signs and does nothing? The choice is yours.

WHO ARE YOU?

As I reflect, I realize that throughout my life, I have encountered four types of individuals. They can be categorized by mind-set levels. Level 1 consists of complacent individuals who can be either negative or positive about their lives. Level 2 consists of motivated but fearful individuals. Level 3 consists of individuals who believe they are their own boss. Which one do you think you are? My goals in this chapter are to get you to recognize your current mind-set, understand why you've bounced back and forth at different life stages, and reset your mind-set. I hope to ignite a spark in you that turns into a massive fire and gets you to a level 3 so you can start to make boss moves.

LEVEL 1

Level 1 individuals are complacent and not motivated to change. This is not necessarily a bad thing. Some people are happy where they are in life and simply do not want to change. Others are not necessarily happy, but they are not willing to change. What they don't realize is that they have put themselves in a box and put limits on their lives. They are letting the fear of the unknown limit their world to only what they see in front of them. You need to show them results before they will believe anything you say. Inadvertently, these individuals cause others to develop feelings of resentment because of their inability of seeing the big picture.

From what I have experienced, many negative level 1 individuals are envious and judgmental, and their level of sincerity is questionable. They may often ask you why you are doing something—mainly just to be nosey or to make arrogant comments, saying they could do the same thing. But it's all talk!

These negative level 1s talk and spread rumors about others to make those individuals look bad. If they complain about their situation, they play the victim and have a low level of accountability. Also, I've observed that they try to keep up with the Joneses, always wanting more material things to show off. Being in the presence of these individuals can be quite draining because of the constant negativity.

You could say, "Good morning; it's a beautiful day today," and this kind of individual would reply, "The sun is shining too brightly today." It seems to me that the highlight of such a person's day is to point out the downside of everything while never offering an encouraging word. You could give these individuals a step-by-step guide to becoming a millionaire and they wouldn't follow it—mostly because they feel like they know everything and have a need to be in control. They would give you every excuse why they shouldn't do it and why it wouldn't work.

Of course, there is absolutely nothing wrong with being content with your current situation. If you are happy and living the life you desire, that's great. There are positive individuals in the level 1 mind-set. They are the opposite of the negative individuals. They don't act envious or judgmental toward others. If they question you about what you're doing, it is to show interest and support.

If you decide to pursue entrepreneurship, go back to school, or transition to a different career, positive level 1 individuals won't have a negative thing to say. However, they may not see themselves as capable of doing anything different from what they have always done. They will support you, but if you aren't careful and strong in your mind-set, they might convince you to stay in your current situation because it's safe there. They have a hard time accepting change—but once they get through a change, they are fine. They will never initiate the change themselves, however, unless they are forced.

If you are, for example, a single mother who has decided to pursue your dream of starting your own business, these positive level 1 individuals will support you. They are very loyal and will be your best customers. These individuals will talk about you, but not in a malicious way. They will talk about all the good things you are doing and your great ideas. They will be the best word-of-mouth advertising for your new business.

These individuals will never complain about their current situations or try to make themselves look better than what they are. A positive level 1 individual is a breath of fresh air compared to a negative complacent person. On the other hand, it can be frustrating because you see potential that the individual isn't willing to pursue. Have you encountered any of these individuals? How do you feel about them?

The funny thing is, the mind-set of negative and positive level 1 individuals when it comes to employment is completely the same; they just react in different ways. The overall mind-set is that you get a job, you work your butt off at that job for thirty years, and then you retire. It doesn't matter to the level 1 individual if you are unappreciated, overworked, and underpaid. To these individuals, you've had steady employment—so this is job security, right?

Well, I don't see the job security in that, and I will tell you why. According to the Merriam-Webster Dictionary, security is the state of being safe and having freedom from worry and anxiety.[3] If you are miserable at your job, witnessing job cuts, or barely making ends meet, there is no security in that. So you tell me: where is the

---

[3] *Merriam-Webster Online*, s.v. "security," accessed June 6, 2017, https://www.merriam-webster.com/dictionary/security.

feeling of being safe and of being free from worry and anxiety in that situation?

Reflection Exercise: If you believe you fit into this level, write down whether you are positive or negative. What are some of the things you do that put you in this level? What moments in life got you here? What current life stage are you in?

_____
_____
_____

LEVEL 2

At level 2, you will find individuals who are very aware of the issues they are not happy with their lives, such as their jobs, finances, or relationships. These individuals don't need any help to think outside the box. The walls are closing in on them, and they want out. They want to change, and they are motivated to change. They have a burning desire to live out their dreams.

Most of these individuals know exactly what they want to do, whether it is starting a business, going back to school to transition into a new career, or climbing their way to the top of the corporate ladder. Others still aren't too sure what they want, simply because they have so many things in their heads they want to do. Although these individuals are outside the box, they are hanging on the edge of it and going nowhere fast.

They just can't seem to take the first step to begin, and they have so many excuses for why they can't do it right now: *I need to wait for the kids to graduate. I'm not financially stable right now. I don't have time. I'm just going to work my job until I retire and then start my business. I'm too old to go back to school.* Excuses, excuses, and more excuses! People, we all have the same twenty-four hours in a day, so it's all in how you choose to spend them. I've learned, and I am sure you will agree, that people make time for what they want to make time for. I know, because that used to be me.

Reflection Exercise: If you believe you fit into this level, write down some of the things you do that put you in this level. What life stage are you currently in? Now write down what is stopping you from moving to the next level.

_____

_____

_____

LEVEL 3

At last we arrive at level 3—the mind-set of being your own boss. Level 3s are movers and shakers. At this level, you no longer just think outside of the box; you take leaps of faith to get yourself as far away from that box as you can in pursuit of your dreams and goals. No excuses.

You walk by faith and not by sight at this level, because it's impossible to know what is around every corner. You push through fear and don't give up when things get rough. You realize that failure is an option and that you are not a failure, because you get up and try again to get results. You prepare, plan, and seek success on your own terms and not by anyone else's.

Your level of optimism increases drastically at this level because of your change in mind-set and the actions you are now taking. You realize that you're not meant to be just an employee, but you will be the employer, the CEO of a Fortune 500 company, the top of your college class, or any other position that you want to be in. At level 3, you will achieve all your dreams, and you will want to change the lives of others.

Some of you may read this and say, "That could never be me." Yet it *can* be you if you want it to be. Some individuals just have this type of mind-set naturally, while others must transition into it. I have a friend who I joke with all the time that he was not meant to be an employee but to be his own boss. He has always known this. His "I am my own boss" mind-set has pushed him to become a very successful real estate broker with his own agency. His personality fits his chosen career path as an entrepreneur.

He still had to go through some of the same things others have experienced—including working for someone else's agency until he could start his own. Like many other entrepreneurs, he didn't give up. What we all should remember is that our beginning is not our ending. All it takes is for you to want it and go get it.

Reflection Exercise: If you believe that you are already at this level, write down the things you did that put you here. Now think back and write down those moments in life that led you in this direction. What are your accomplishments? What are you striving to achieve?

_____
_____
_____

WHO WAS I?

Even as a child, I had the "I am my own boss" mind-set. I have always had dreams, but life just kept getting in the way. My dream was to climb the corporate ladder, but as soon as I got my first accounting job, I realized I was never meant to be an employee. The seed had already been planted in me to be my own boss. I just had to figure out how to nurture it, grow it, and bring it to fruition. Had I not figured it out, you would not be reading this book.

I was raised to try new things, to be ambitious, and to let my creative juices flow. I was taught I could be whatever I wanted to be by being a leader, not a follower. Never was I told *no* about any activity

I wanted to try, which kept me thinking outside the box and trying new things, even as an adult. However, I got stuck in safe mode after being hit by the following bricks thrown at me, some thanks to my own poor decision-making:

- My grandmother died when I was young. I asked why God would take her from me. She was the one who taught me to have faith and trust in God. I lost that when she died. Thank God, I still had my mother, or I would've been a complete wreck.
- When I went away to college, one of my uncles passed away. I wanted to follow his footsteps, so I chose to go to his alma mater. He was one of my biggest fans. When he died, the desire to continue in college stopped. I questioned why God would take away these two people who I felt played such a tremendous role in my life.
- I became pregnant while still in college, and I quit school. I didn't care; I didn't want to be there anyway. That was my mind-set at that stage in my life. However, I immediately fell in love for the first time in my life with my son. I then settled in a rebound relationship that I thought would fill the void of my deceased grandmother and uncle.
- The next year, I became pregnant with my second son. I fell in love for the second time in my life with him. However, I was miserable in a relationship, and for a short time I became a negative complacent individual. I only held on to this relationship because I felt so much had been taken from me already.

Brick after brick. I felt like a failure. I kept all that bottled up and did not share my feelings with anyone. I just pushed everyone away.

One day, I looked at my two precious angels and decided enough was enough. They were all the motivation I needed to no longer allow anyone or anything to be a distraction in my life. No more feeling sorry for myself. I was not raised to be like this or to question God.

It became clear to me that everything I thought I had lost with the death of my grandmother and uncle never went away. I had allowed those human emotions of fear, pain, and grief to take over. They grew into weeds that overpowered the seeds that had been planted in me as a child. I lost the desire to continue to nurture and grow those seeds, yet they never died. I thought I was alone, but God never left me.

My sons were a wake-up call from God. I also had friends, family, and people I called family in my life who loved and supported me. I always had the support system; I just chose not to tap into it. But eventually, I took those very bricks that were thrown at me and used them to build a foundation to elevate me. I transformed my mind-set and went back to school, got married, moved to a new city, and began climbing the corporate ladder. I started my journey to being my own boss. I did not care how long it took for me to achieve all my dreams; I was going to do it one step at a time.

I first knew I wanted to start my own business when I went back to school to pursue my bachelor's degree. The course content, along with the assignments and professors, sparked so many interests and ideas, and brought out skills I didn't know I had. Unsure of what I should do, I decided to get a job. My plan was to climb the corporate ladder and gain as much experience as I could in different areas related to my business and accounting degrees. But I never found that ideal position I wanted to remain in. So, like a good employee, I made myself stay in positions for one to three years, and then I moved on. I did this to maintain a good work history.

Years went by. The more I pushed the thought of starting my own business aside, the more frustrated I got. I knew switching from job to job was only a short-term fix for my frustration. I dreaded getting up in the morning to go clock in. Don't get me wrong: I worked for some great companies. At one point, I even thought I'd found my ideal job. But I still wasn't happy. I then realized it was me. It didn't matter where I worked; the only thing that was going to satisfy me was to literally be my own boss.

It was time to revisit the idea of starting my own business. I thought that perhaps I could start a tax and bookkeeping business. Great idea! I had all these years of accounting experience in different industries—private, public, government, education, and health care. After writing a complete business plan, however, I no longer desired to start that business or work in accounting anymore at all. I didn't want to start a business that was the same job I'd held for all these years.

My business plan was the turning point. All this time, I had been focused on figuring out what I wanted to do. I didn't realize that all I had to do was take the time to figure out what I *didn't* want to do. It's just like when you go out to eat with family or friends and no one knows what to eat. But soon as someone gives a suggestion, you quickly say, "Oh no, I don't want that." You could get to an agreement sooner if you decided what you didn't want first.

I had to stop and reevaluate a lot of things. My mind was a mess. I was clearly traveling down the wrong road. I had ignored all the signs, refused to ask for direction, and made excuses for it. I was out of the box, but I realized that for me to take that leap of faith, I had to come up with the right plan. I had to change my mind-set again to get to where I really wanted to be.

It was important to be crystal clear, in everything I wanted to do, about how I wanted to start and how everything was going to be linked together. The hardest part was fighting through the fear of taking the first step to start my first business, Shanelle & Co. Boutique. Once I did, I wondered what the heck took me so long.

I know some of you may be shocked by my business decision. But my boutique was something I wanted to give 200 percent to, no matter what. I figured that just because I had these degrees didn't mean I had to start a business related to them. My degrees gave me the know-how to start and run a business. And the rest is history.

THERE'S MORE TO BEING YOUR OWN BOSS

Being a boss is not just about owning a business. It's about being successful in all areas of your life. Although I was taking the necessary steps to start my own business, there was something missing. I was still a full-time employee when I started my online business, and becoming a part-time entrepreneur was not my vision. Then the light bulb came on. To successfully transition from employee to employer, I couldn't just focus on my career choices. There were other areas—finances, relationships, personal well-being—that needed a mind-set shift too.

The way my vision was, there was no way I could stay an employee. I knew that God had given me this vision, so if I kept the faith, trusted him, and did the work, it would all fall into place. Not only did God give me a vision for my career, he gave me the road map. I knew it was time for me to be a history-maker and formulate this plan to share with others who desired change in their lives.

The road map that lies within the pages of this book will empower you to change your mind-set and accomplish your career dreams. If you are sick and tired of being an employee, get ready to change your mind-set. Get ready to create and implement an action plan to achieve your dreams. The million-dollar question is: are you going to continue to stay in your current mind-set? If you're up for the challenge and willing to commit, you can and will be your own boss. It won't happen overnight, nor will it be easy. If you're ready, there is only one thing left for you to do, and that's put it in writing.

Throughout life, I'm sure you've been told not to be a quitter or never to give up. To truly be a boss, you must quit and give up some things. You must give up negative thoughts, excuses, toxic relationships, and any distractions that bring stress to your life. Now that we are clear on that, if you're ready to commit, put down your first "I quit" date.

PLEDGE OF COMMITMENT
On this day, _____, I commit to quit and give up my current mind-set to transition to the "I am my own boss" mind-set. No more negativity, excuses, toxic relationships, hindrances from achieving my dreams, or anything that brings stress to my life. Today is the day I quit to begin to live.

CHAPTER 2

GETTING BACK ON THE RIGHT PATH

Congratulations! You have taken the first step in transitioning to the "I am my own boss" mind-set. No longer will you accept the limits others have put on your life. No longer will you wake up each day to build someone else's dreams. You have made the commitment to build your own dreams and give up all the distractions holding you back. So what now? Well, it's time to get you prepared for this journey. Please do not skim through this book. It is meant for you to read it in its entirety and complete all the exercises.

As with any other trip you have been on, it is very important to get oriented and prepare for what is ahead of you. You pack your supplies, and then you check your map or GPS to see the highways and exits along the way; check the traffic; determine rest stops; and estimate your arrival time. So here is a quick overview of your trip through this book. There are three sections, each of which represents a phase of coming out of a life storm. Divided among the sections are my six strategies to guide you on this journey. This is a blueprint for life after your mind-set shift.

SECTION I: IN THE MIDST OF A STORM

STRATEGY 1: BRAINSTORMING

Here in section I, you will apply my first strategy for transforming your mind-set. We are going to brainstorm ways to bring you out of your life storm. In the business world, brainstorming is a relaxed and informal approach to problem-solving. It encourages people to come up with thoughts and ideas that can, at first, seem a bit crazy. Some of these ideas can be crafted into original, creative solutions to a problem, while others spark even more ideas.

Brainstorming gets people out of their normal way of thinking. You will take a personal inventory of yourself to figure out exactly what career dreams you want or don't want to pursue, why you haven't started, and how you are going to start. This is a judgment-free zone in which you can declutter your mind and collect all those bricks that life has thrown at you. This strategy will force you to be honest with yourself. No more excuses!

SECTION II: RAINY DAYS

STRATEGY 2: RESEARCHING

In this section, we'll discuss the importance of taking the time to educate yourself before you jump into action. You will seek direction on this journey within yourself and with outside resources. You will learn several effective and efficient tips to prepare you in your research.

This is where you'll start to make sense of what you really want to do by learning more of what it takes to get it done. You may find that because of your research, there is something you initially did not want to pursue but now you do—and vice versa. Also, we'll address time management to evaluate how you utilize your time.

Most importantly, we'll look at how researching helps you to set some realistic goals.

STRATEGY 3: PLANNING
We've done the prep work with the brainstorming and researching strategies. The hard part is over. The storm is easing up to just some rainy days. We'll now focus on planning. Here is where you will create the framework and start building your foundation with all those bricks that were thrown at you. We will further explore your dreams, discuss mind-set makeover tips, learn how to set goals, and begin to create your action plans and exit strategies.

STRATEGY 4: IMPLEMENTING
Now you are completely thinking outside the box. You are standing on the edge with your eyes on your prize. You've laid a solid foundation through the brainstorming, researching, and planning exercises. We're now at the point you have been waiting for: Finally, you get the chance to take that leap of faith.

You should now understand why creating a foundation and blueprint for your vision was necessary before you acted. You are armed with the proper tools to weather any storm. When obstacles get in your way, you won't get knocked off course. We will discuss how you should document your efforts to monitor your progress and develop a reward system for the small accomplishments along the way.

SECTION III: SUNNY DAYS

STRATEGY 5: EVALUATING
Up to this point, you have been discussing, strategizing, and implementing your strategic plans to achieve your dreams. Here, you will evaluate your action plans to see if what you are doing is working.

You've already been documenting your efforts, so you are ahead of the game. It will be easy to adjust if you need to make any revisions.

STRATEGY 6: LIVING

We'll conclude with the secret to living and experiencing great joy and self-fulfillment. The more changes you achieve, the fewer limits your mind-set will put on your life. You will feel empowered and know that even if you aren't the next billionaire, your quality of life is much better than before.

Everyone's definition of success is different. You're not trying to keep up with the Joneses. Nor are you here to criticize what others are doing. Changing your life and mind-set will create options for you that weren't present before. You are your own boss, and you will know how to remain a boss for the rest of your life.

Now that you know what the six strategies are to becoming your own boss, what do you think? Be honest. Do you think it will be too hard, or do you still feel like you aren't ready? I'm sure you are ready, for two reasons: First, you are reading this book. Second, you already made the commitment; now it's time to go through the process.

This journey will not be the same for everyone. You have to figure out what works best for you based on your life stages and apply these strategies accordingly. What life stage are you at: single, married, parent, grandparent, in your twenties, in your thirties, close to retirement? Now, if you're ready, let the journey begin!

CHAPTER 3

CALMING THE STORM

When going through a life storm, your emotions are all over the place. Your mind is cluttered. You desperately need to figure out what you want to pursue and determine what your distractions are. I hope you are excited and ready to get out of this life storm. You may feel a little nervous or anxious, but that's a natural reaction to change. First on our agenda is for you to take a personal inventory of all your thoughts and get them organized.

It is important for you to get everything out of your mind and onto paper. This is your judgment-free zone. You must be honest with yourself for this to work. Declutter your mind like you spring-clean to declutter your home. Grab a pen and a notebook. The first thing I want you to do is make a simple list to start organizing your thoughts. Write down every career dream you've ever thought about pursuing. Leave some space in between the entries.

Now that you have your list, take a minute to evaluate and write below each item why you want to pursue it and what is stopping you. Even if you think these things are insignificant, they could be playing a huge role in your life that you didn't even realize. Again, I want to stress the importance of being honest with yourself. This is not the time to be in denial about things going on in your life.

You may have something on your list only because someone else thought it was a good idea for you—just as I did when I planned to start a tax preparation and bookkeeping business because others thought it seemed logical for me. When I was honest with myself, I learned that I didn't want to do accounting period, as a job or a business. That quickly got crossed off my list, along with a few other items. I eventually narrowed my list down to eight.

This evaluation will get you to what you really want to do faster. Without it, you will waste valuable time working on something you're never going to finish if you didn't want to do it from the beginning. Best you weed those items out now and cross them off your list. Time is precious. If lost, you can't get it back. Please use it wisely!

We will now take what is left on your list and prioritize. There is no way you can do everything at once. You may think you can, but trust me, you will overwhelm yourself and not get anything accomplished.

I don't want you to give up on this journey, so you need to take this one step at a time. Carefully identify what is most important to you and start working on first, second, third, and so on. You may find that you can work on some items simultaneously. Take your time and think about this. Once you have decided, you should number each item.

When I first did this brainstorm exercise, I had a list so long it looked like a grocery list. It seemed a little ridiculous at the time, but these were all the things I wanted to do. I had so many business ventures I wanted to pursue, and I didn't know where to start. So I didn't do anything for a long time. Nothing made sense until I put it all down on paper. That put into perspective what I was unwilling to do because it would not be beneficial for me or my family.

For instance, I was not willing to go back to college to get another degree to pursue a career within a different industry. I wanted to be an entrepreneur, not an employee. I had enough degrees. For anything else I needed to know, I could research, teach myself, or attend a seminar.

Also, getting another degree would create more debt. One of my goals was to be debt-free, so again, going back to school did not make sense for me. Not to mention, I just did not have the time or patience to go back to school. However, I was willing to take a short course to get a certification or license that would be beneficial to one of my business ventures. This led me into getting my real estate broker license.

There is one last thing you need to do to your list: write beside each item how you think you are going to get started with it. You don't have to know all the details right now. We will get into that part a little later. For instance, say you want to open a boutique. How are you going to do that? Are you going to open a storefront business or operate online? Be as specific as you can for each item.

Congratulations on decluttering your mind! I'm sure some uncertainty may have been stirred up while creating and evaluating your list—especially when you wrote down what was stopping you from pursuing your dreams. Were any of your reasons related to your finances, relationships, or personal well-being? You need money for a start-up. If you are already living paycheck to paycheck, where are you going to get the money to start a business? Are you in a relationship with someone who is not supportive? Is your stress level extremely high? What are your thoughts toward your current employer? These are areas that need to be evaluated to change your mind-set. They are all related to the chance of your career dreams becoming reality.

We'll take a closer look at those four specific areas—career, relationships, finance, and personal well-being—in the next chapter. For now, you have started to put things in order and will soon reach a mind-set level that gives you peace.

II

RAINY DAYS

Strategy 2: Researching
Strategy 3: Planning
Strategy 4: Implementing

CHAPTER 4

ASKING FOR DIRECTIONS

Do the best you can until you know better.
Then when you know better, do better.
—*Maya Angelou*

How difficult is it for you to ask for directions when you're lost? Simply stop what you are doing and ask someone, read the instructions, or do a little research, right? In life, when you hit a bump in the road, it may not be that simple. Your mindset can have you so far gone on the wrong path you keep trying to figure things out for yourself without seeking any directions. That was something I could relate to until I changed to an "I am my own boss" mind-set. Now is the time for you to commit to strategy 2: Researching.

LET'S RESEARCH
The research strategy will show you which direction to take to reach your goals. It is necessary to take the time to educate yourself on some things before you jump into your action plan. You will seek

direction for this journey ahead of you within yourself and through outside resources.

Let's consider a thirty-three-year-old single woman without children who works full-time. She does the brainstorming exercise and realizes she wants to start her own day care. Not only does she want to own it, she wants to be the acting director of the facility. Because of her babysitting experience from the time she was thirteen years old; her love for kids; and the fact that kids are just naturally drawn to her, she believes this is the right decision. In addition, she has the same workforce frustrations as everyone else.

However, there are a few things stopping her. First, she doesn't know where to begin. Second, she knows nothing about running a business. Third, she doesn't know where she would get the funding for her business. And fourth, she has family members and friends suggesting that it's not a good idea.

To get more direction on how to achieve this dream, she does some basic research. She first finds out that she needs to go back to school to get her early childhood degree. She can simultaneously take a few business classes and attend some business seminars. Also, by speaking with other day care owners, banks, and government agencies, she discovers there are all types of resources and funding options available.

So, with some basic research, she finds out how to do the very things that were stopping her from pursuing her dream. It looks like this individual is getting things in perspective and changing her mind-set to be her own boss. Now she needs to do more specific research to figure out the school she will attend, what the program consists of, how long it lasts, and if there are any accelerated programs available to enable her to finish more quickly.

The way this individual did her research is the same way you will do yours. Research is a tool that will help you to overcome the things that are holding you back and get you started. We will discuss dealing with the naysayers in your life in a later chapter.

FUNDAMENTALS

Whether you realize it or not, you have been to corners of your mind with these exercises that you haven't traveled to before. What you needed was a new perspective and to put some order to those thoughts in your head. Let's keep this mind-set-transformation ball rolling by discussing a few things that will help you with your research. You don't have to reinvent the wheel. There is an enormous amount of information available about what you want to do.

Think of someone you admire—a successful person you would want to model yourself after related to your business venture or someone who already has that boss mind-set to motivate you. If you don't know of anyone, just use Google, and I am sure you will find someone. The Internet will be your best friend. All the information you need to get the details to make your dreams a reality is at your fingertips. Find articles, books, and magazines on your interests and other topics to elevate your level of thinking. If you have limited time, try to listen to audiobooks or watch videos. You can find just about anything on YouTube. I sure did!

Don't limit yourself to the Internet or books. Get out there and talk to people who are doing what you want to do. The more you know, the more you grow into a boss. You will never find yourself trapped in a box ever again. Use all these resources to learn more before you fully commit to your action plan. By the time you are done, you will have a massive amount of knowledge and ideas to start your action plan.

I wrote this book to share my story and the knowledge I acquired on my own journey. I know for a fact that change starts with your mind-set. If you continue to do the same thing, you will always get the same result. You must change the way you think and the people you look at. Study successful people to learn what they all have in common. Study unsuccessful people—what do *they* all have in common? (Spoiler alert: it's their mind-set.) Look at the people around you. What do you see?

Watch relatable videos, read books or magazines, follow individuals on social media, go to seminars, and seek out anything that will educate you. These are the fundamentals of your research. Apply what makes sense to your situation. You can't follow the actions of a millionaire if you are not a millionaire—meaning you should follow the steps the millionaire, successful entrepreneur, CEO, or best-selling author took to get there. The journey will be different for you even if you are taking the same steps. Remember: we all walk different paths through life.

BUSINESS LESSON #1: LEGAL BUSINESS STRUCTURES

Before we go any further, let me give you a quick business lesson on how to research the direction you will take to start your own business. I did not include this lesson at the back of the book with the rest because this is something you need to know now. When starting a business, it is very important to create the correct business structure based on the ownership, liability, and taxation of your business. Always consult with an accounting professional about the tax implications for the structure you choose. The legal business structures are sole proprietorship, partnership, corporation, and limited-liability corporation (LLC).

Sole proprietorship is probably the most common structure among new entrepreneurs because it is the simplest to set up and maintain. You are the sole person who owns and operates the business. A *partnership* is the simplest legal structure when there are two or more owners involved in the business. However, for both unincorporated structures, you as the owners are personally liable for everything. Basically, if you get sued, your personal assets are at stake.

The legal business structures that separate your business from your personal life are *corporations* and *LLCs*. A corporation is a legal entity that handles all the responsibilities of the organization, while an LLC is a hybrid structure that allows owners to take advantage of the benefits of both a corporation and a sole proprietorship or partnership.

LLCs are becoming a popular structure for entrepreneurs because personal liability is removed, as with corporations. At the same time, the taxation of profits and losses is treated the same way as a sole proprietorship or partnership, offering the best of both worlds. However, be aware that it is costlier to set up an LLC or corporation versus a sole proprietorship or partnership. I would say it is money well spent to be able to protect your personal assets in the event of a lawsuit against your business.

My advice to you would be to add this to you list to research. Consult with a professional to see what works best for you. Consider free or low-cost professional assistance from your local small business center, the Small Business Administration, a business attorney, or another professional. If you are strapped for cash, start with one of the simple structures, and then you can incorporate later. Apply for an employer identification number (EIN) with the IRS instead of using your social security number. Open a separate business bank account with your EIN.

It is crucial that you go ahead and get in a mind-set to separate your personal and business affairs. If you start off building a credible business, it will be easier to transition to another legal structure, such as an LLC.

IS THAT WHAT I REALLY WANT?

> *You can always find a job, but you only get one chance at your dreams.*
> —Bill Bellamy

Now is the time for you to seek direction beyond the obvious external resources. Dig further within yourself to get a clearer understanding of what it is you truly want. We need to address your likes and dislikes, your strengths and weaknesses, and your skills and character traits. This exercise will confirm if your dreams and goals are likely to become a reality—and also ensure that you aren't just coming up with quick fixes to get out of your current situation. No tricks here: this is strictly about you.

Go back to your notebook and review your career and business choices. Write down your likes and dislikes. If you love to talk to and interact with people, list that. If you are shy and prefer not to be in the spotlight, list that. If what you list as a business requires you to be in front of a crowd all the time and you don't like to do that, then you may want to rethink that particular career choice.

Next, make a list of your skills. What is it that you can do? In what area do you have experience? Make a list of your character traits. Are you creative and organized? Do you analyze everything? Do you have an eye for detail? Are you an outdoors person?

Last, you will need to create a list of your strengths and weaknesses. It's important to know what you are good at and what you are not. Just because you like something does not mean you are good at it. Just because you can do something doesn't mean you like doing it.

These probably sound like interview questions to you. Well, go ahead and interview yourself. Would you hire you? As an entrepreneur, you will start off wearing all the hats in your business. Are you ready for that? Are you qualified? Do you know when you need to ask for help? You will later learn more in-depth that being a successful entrepreneur doesn't mean you know it all. The secret is to create the right team to assist you.

You may be thinking that as a start-up, you can't afford to hire or acquire certain professional services. Well, this is where you need to be resourceful. Do some research to locate free and low-cost services in your community, virtual assistants, or freelancers online. Utilize the students and professors at your local community college or university. Students are always in need of a way to build their résumé prior to graduation. Also, ask friends or family to volunteer to assist you until you can hire someone. Again, research to see what is available to you to make your business venture successful.

Let's keep this momentum going by continuing the research within yourself. We will take a closer look at how your career, relationships, finances, and personal health are directly related to your current mind-set. Being your own boss is about having everything together as a whole, not just in one area of your life. We will evaluate and change your mind-set in each area to make your vision come full circle.

FOUR QUARTERS MAKE A WHOLE MIND-SET

FIRST QUARTER: CAREER

Obviously, you are not happy with your current career situation, and you want more out of life. That feeling haunted me for years. In my research, I came across many articles, books, and interviews with different entrepreneurs, and the common factor was their mind-set. Some made the decision to take that leap and give up the frustrating nine-to-five to pursue their dreams, while others were pushed into their entrepreneurial mind-set because either they or their spouse lost their job; they became homeless; or they were, for whatever reason, forced into it.

Don't wait to be put in a situation where you have no choice but to take action. Take the leap on your own terms. Work through all the anger and frustration you feel to create a more positive outlook toward your current employment situation. Use that frustration to fuel your motivation to get to your dream destination.

Your attitude will determine how far you go on this journey. Try to determine your mood each morning. Make the decision that you will have a great day before it begins. At your current place of employment, don't let someone or something make you upset when you already know it is coming; you just don't know when. I know that is easier said than done, but you can't let others control you. You control your actions, and doing these next two things will make each day a little easier to get through until you quit that job.

First, stop making your life revolve around your job. If you have vacation time, use it. Don't go years or months without taking time off. You need an opportunity to spend time with family, to vacation, or to recharge yourself mentally and physically. The prolonged day-to-day stress of your job will make you a negative and miserable individual. I never let my life revolve around a job because I refuse to. I know others who have, and it's sad. My choice was for my life to revolve around my family and my personal interests. Don't let a doctor's appointment or needing to paint your house be the only reason you take a day off.

Second, change your terminology when talking about your job. Your employer will refer to you as a full-time permanent employee with an ID number. But from here on out, we are going to refer to your job as your temporary assignment. Get out of the mind-set of being employed long-term. You are temporarily assigned there as you prepare to start your business or transition into your dream career—not to retire.

When you were in school, you didn't stay in a course until you graduated. You completed your assigned coursework and received a grade. Sometimes you needed to switch courses because it just wasn't working for you. Think of your job now as a temporary assignment that is preparing you for the next level, just as if you were in school. Instead of receiving grades, you are compensated with a paycheck. Sometimes it takes a couple of assignments to pull out of us what is needed to prepare us for owning a business or being in our dream career.

We will no longer say "your job" or "my job" in this book or speak it out loud. This is not your job, and you are not going to work. You are on assignment to be compensated for your time spent at the company. You will give it your all, even when you don't feel like it, because that is what bosses do. After all, this is temporary. You won't be there too much longer!

Along with changing your mind-set toward your current assignment, there are a few rules you must follow to be a boss. Regardless of whether you want to be an entrepreneur or your dream career is to be a sports agent, these rules apply to you.

1. Invest in yourself. Yes, I mean with time and money. If you aren't willing to, then don't expect anyone else to either. Buy that power suit to give yourself a boost of confidence when going to meetings, networking, or interviewing. Attend that seminar or take that course to learn something for your business or dream career. When you invest in yourself, you create value in yourself. You should always get 100 percent return on your investment.

2. Invest in your dream. Do this with both your time and your money. Remember, this is your dream and your vision. Nurture it and bring it to life so others can see what you see. If you are not willing to sacrifice to invest in your own dream, then no one else is going to take you seriously. Despite what you may have heard, you do have to spend money to make money. Nothing in life is free. Everything has a cost. Whether it's you or someone else bearing the cost of a free item or service, someone must pay for it. I learned in my college economics course that there's no such thing as a free lunch. You may have to get creative, but you must invest in your dream so your customers, clients, or investors will invest as well.

3. Create your own opportunities. Don't wait for things to come to you or have a pity party when someone tells you no. Get out there and make things happen. By investing in yourself and your dreams, you create enough value in what you have to offer that others will notice you. Put your foot down and stop being overlooked for advancement. Acquire a career you can excel at and be happy in. Create your own company and do things your way.

4. Stay ready. If you *stay* ready, you never need to *get* ready when an opportunity arises. Although you are at the starting point of transitioning your career, you need to always be prepared. Keep your résumé up to date, have a business plan, and keep your contact information readily accessible to hand out. Business cards or brochures are very inexpensive for networking. Before I started my own business, I always kept my résumé current. Even if I had just started a new job, I kept it current. I also updated my written business plan as my businesses evolved. I was prepared for a networking opportunity or to create an opportunity for myself. Stay ready so when it is go time, you won't miss your opportunity.

5. Use your time wisely. I know this rule may sound a little elementary, but as adults, sometimes we lose sight of the basics. We all have the same twenty-four hours in a day as everyone else. We often say we don't have time, but we really do. When you have a full-time assignment, a family, and activities outside of your household, there must be a balance. Time is one thing you cannot get back, so use it wisely.

Your mind-set must be that your time is precious, so you need to limit what you spend it on. Shift your time on your computer, laptop, tablet, iPad, or smartphone from playing games, shopping, or socializing on social media to researching, planning, implementing, networking, and promoting your next career move. Use every free moment to be productive without neglecting your family and other responsibilities. Sacrifice going out with your friends and stay home to work on your business. Use your lunch break at your current assignment to get things done.

Choose to make sacrifices now so you can live the life you want to live. Stay focused and look straight ahead. Don't look to the left, right, or behind you. Keep your eyes on the prize. You can't change the past, so focus on the present to better your future. I don't know about you, but I would rather make the necessary sacrifices now to later live the life I've always dreamed of. Are you willing to do the same?

6. **Invest in others**. I believe we all have a responsibility to the community we live in. We should invest time, money, or knowledge in others. My grandmother used to tell me that this is how you get your blessings. What may seem small to you may be huge to someone else. You probably do this all the time for family, friends, coworkers, church, or in your community. It isn't necessary to broadcast everything you do, and at times your efforts may go unrecognized, but don't let that deter you. Take the knowledge, experiences, and resources you gain from investing in yourself and your dreams to invest in others.

There are so many things you can do to invest in others. Mentor someone, support another small business, support a youth sports team, donate to a charity, host a charity fundraiser, volunteer, support a local cause, teach someone something instead of doing it for them, etc. Whether it's big or small, just do it! Investing in others is rewarding.

We will get more into evaluating your career goals and creating a plan for you to implement to get to the next level. No more looking back and focusing on the could-haves or should-haves. It's all about the here and now and what you are becoming.

If you get, give. If you learn, teach.
—*Maya Angelou*

SECOND QUARTER: RELATIONSHIPS

Your family, friends, significant others, and partners are the people who have the most impact on your life. They often think they know you better than you know yourself. But truth be told, they won't know the real you if you don't show or tell them. Sometimes you don't even know yourself. It's important to recognize who has your best interest at heart. Some you may have known since you were younger—cousins who you grew up with—or maybe a coworker becomes a great friend. No matter how long the relationship has existed, that person should be there to provide support, stability, and love.

Often, these individuals cause us the most stress. All some do is take, take, take, and they never contribute anything to the relationship. We tend to stay in these one-sided relationships to spare the feelings of others, even if it causes us pain. As you transform into a boss, carefully evaluate your relationships. It may be best to limit your interaction with some while cutting all ties to those with a crab mentality.

Don't limit yourself to who you have always known. Explore

new relationships and network with others. Surround yourself with people who genuinely motivate, support, and elevate you so that you can reciprocate. Don't block your blessings by holding onto someone who might hinder your progress or by turning away the person God sent to answer your prayers.

Consider your more intimate relationships with spouses or partners. Do you get love, support, and motivation from them as well? If you don't have a healthy relationship, this can be a touchy subject. These are all things you need to consider, because all have an impact on your mind-set. I'm no relationship expert, but if your situation turns toxic, you need to get out fast. I've been in a toxic relationship before, and it will break you down. The last thing on your mind would be to start a business or seek out your dream job.

Family situations sometimes arise where you become the sole caretaker of a sick parent, spouse, child, or sibling. This type of situation is not one you can run out on. Don't be too proud to ask for help. You may need someone other than a friend or family member to talk to. Or you may need some additional help in caring for your family member.

Many times, we don't utilize the available resources that would give us the help we need. If you feel like you have reached a breaking point, please seek out the necessary help from a therapist, pastor, domestic violence counselor, etc. Again, if you have all this going on, you will not be focused on any career plans.

THIRD QUARTER: PERSONAL

Often, we are so focused on taking care of everyone else that we forget how important it is to take care of ourselves. In all our time-management efforts, we manage to leave out time for ourselves. We neglect our personal wants, needs, health, and well-being. I did this until I realized that if I didn't take care of myself first, I wouldn't be any good for anyone else. It is very important for you to go to the doctor regularly for preventative checkups, get enough sleep, create some me time, eat healthier, and exercise regularly. By changing a few habits and multitasking, you can use your time wisely while looking out for yourself.

I suggest you learn to say no. It may be hard at first, but trust me: it gets easier the more you say it. You can create time for yourself by not taking on the extra responsibilities. Try waking up early to exercise or complete a few tasks to free up time during the day to do something else. You could opt to take a walk and listen to an audiobook that you can't find the time to read. This will help you unwind and exercise at the same time. If you are really looking for some quality me time, make it part of your schedule. A spa day is guaranteed to relax and rejuvenate you.

Plan to cook more at home and eat healthier. Try turning dinnertime into a fun family activity by including your kids or significant other. Even with a busy schedule, you can conserve time by fixing quick meals that will provide leftovers for the next day's lunch or dinner. Yes, eating out is convenient, but it's not always the most cost effective or healthy choice. If necessary, consult a nutritionist to help you improve your eating habits and to recommend some healthy recipes. In addition, please consult your physician about your diet or exercise plans if you have any preexisting health conditions.

Finally, work on growing spiritually. I'm not here to sway you to one faith or another. But speaking for myself, I willingly chose to seek God, and I began to get a true sense of peace. My increasing faith led me to trust God, not man. I learned to trust God even when I didn't understand his plan for me.

I recall a promotion that I didn't get that I thought was well-deserved. Yes, I was upset at the time, but not getting the promotion turned out to be a blessing. That position evolved into something that nobody wanted—not even the person who was promoted. I thank God for not opening that door for me.

I also thank God for delivering me from my fear of taking these leaps of faith in life. I know God has been there for my family, friends, and I through so many situations. When I can't explain how a situation played out the way it did, I just look up to the sky and say, "I know this was nothing but you, God." You know, I pray that my family and I are covered by the blood of Jesus and with the whole armor of God every day before we leave the house. And so I say to you, if you have tried everything else and nothing seems to work, try God.

FOURTH QUARTER: FINANCES

Your finances are the second major focus of your mind-set makeover. There are many myths and misconceptions about money that play a major factor in your mind-set on that topic. When you were growing up, how was money handled in your household? What did your parents or grandparents teach or not teach you about money? What do you hear others say about money? What do you wish you had done or not done with your money?

Money is a very touchy subject to discuss in many households. Some people think, *I work hard for my money, so I should spend it on what I want when I want*—especially if they didn't have much growing up. Others believe it's wrong to have a lot of money. A close friend and I had a conversation about that very thing. My friend shared some thoughts with me as to how it made her feel uncomfortable to have a lot of money. Living paycheck to paycheck had become her norm and comfort zone. I shared how I saw money as a resource to provide me with an abundant life, a sense of security, options, and the ability to provide opportunities for others.

Is it wrong to be rich? It depends on who you ask. In my opinion, there is nothing wrong with wanting or being rich. But in the mind-set of being your own boss, you should want to not just be rich but to create wealth. When I think of being rich, I think of boastful and frivolous spending. But when I think of wealth, I think of someone building and creating a legacy that others benefit from too.

Personally, it's not whether having money is wrong, it's what you choose to do with it. Regardless of how you feel about it, there is one thing for sure that we can all agree on: you can't live without it. We no longer live in a time where we can barter for goods and services. The majority of our transactions involve the exchange of currency. You can't go to the grocery store and trade a used shirt for some canned goods.

If you truly want to be an entrepreneur, you must change every aspect of your mind-set dealing with finances, from the amount of income you bring in to your spending habits and your savings methods. How do you feel about money? If you have children, what do you teach them about money? What do you need to do to avoid the debt trap? Mastering your finances is going to be extremely hard, but it can be done. Start with your personal finances, and let those good practices roll over into your business finances.

Don't believe the hype about being able to start and maintain a business with no money. At some point, you are going to have to invest in yourself and your business for people to take you seriously. Sure, there are a few exceptions to the rule, but we are not going to focus on them. If you are currently a full-time employee, you already have your first investor: your employer. You just need to figure out how to get your personal finances on track to allocate a small amount to funding your business. This seed money is necessary to start and structure a credible business. From there, you can build business credit to grow your company, and then you will no longer need the funds from that investor.

We will talk more about evaluating your finances and creating a financial plan in later chapters. I'm not going to give you the exact chapter, because I don't want you skipping ahead. Wouldn't you like to get out of debt, create more income streams, and start your business? Well, you will need all the information in between to do that.

CHAPTER 5

QUICK SYSTEMS CHECK— PREPARING FOR YOUR JOURNEY

If you don't like something change it. If you can't change it, change your attitude.
—Maya Angelou

The prep work is done, and you are ready to begin the journey out of your storm. Your life storm isn't going to pass on its own. You must walk through the rain and go through the process to overcome it. You have brainstormed and researched, so things should be starting to look a little clearer now. But as with any trip you are preparing for, you should do one final check before you hit the road. That is exactly what we are going to do in this chapter. I have created an eight-point mind-set makeover checkpoint system for you to complete in its entirety before you take the leap. Let's get to it, because I know you are anxious to get started.

CHECKPOINT #1: OVERCOME YOUR FEARS

It's hard to come out of your comfort zone to do something different when you fear the unknown. You worry about the what-ifs instead of taking action. There is no way to know what is around every corner, so you must rely on your faith. According to Hebrews 11:1 (KJV), "faith is the substance of things hoped for, the evidence of things not seen." Let go of what was or what is and have faith in what will be. Trust me, the more you use your faith, the stronger it gets. The only fear you should have is the fear of God. Let your faith be bigger than your fear.

CHECKPOINT #2: KNOW THAT FAILURE IS AN OPTION

Even the best of the best have been rejected or failed at something—multiple times. They are successful because they tried again. Stop giving up when something doesn't work the first time. Continue to try until you reach your breakthrough moment.

You may have to take a different approach, but don't give up easily. Winning is what you do when you come back from failing. I tell myself daily that even when I lose, I win, because my faith will teach me to fly every time.

CHECKPOINT #3: CREATE A SUPPORT TEAM

Be around like-minded people who help you stay focused on achieving your goals. It's always good to have someone or something to throw you a lifeline of positivity when you hit a bump in the road. Your support team doesn't have to be made up of people you know. It can be a social media group, a resource center, a life or business coach, or a church group. Whoever you choose, be sure they are going to hold you accountable for your actions.

Even as an entrepreneur, you will need a great team to assist you in carrying out your vision—a small, qualified, and highly effective and efficient group of people to take some of the weight off your shoulders. Your team does not need to be individuals you know, and they do not need to have the same qualities as you. They just need to be qualified in the area in which you need them to get the job done. Some people think you should be an expert at it all to be a boss. Not true! You are a boss because you know when to allow someone else to do it for you. Create a description of duties and then seek out that person to add to your team.

CHECKPOINT #4: CREATE SELF-MOTIVATIONAL MOMENTS
Stop sabotaging yourself by speaking negativity into the universe about yourself and your situation. Life and death lies in the power of your tongue. Good or bad, you can speak it into existence. Don't constantly say "My kids are bad" and expect them to be good. Don't say "I'll never be able to have my own business" and expect to be your own boss. Your attitude, the words you speak, your actions, and your reactions all determine whether you will have a positive or negative outcome in your daily activities and relationships.

Find some simple ways to change your negatives into positives. Listen to music, receive inspirational e-mails, read inspirational quotes, or chant an inspirational affirmation or Bible verse. Remember, self-motivation is key. You cannot depend on others to motivate you.

CHECKPOINT #5: DON'T BELIEVE THE HYPE
You can't believe everything you hear and see. Do your own research and figure out what makes sense for you and your family. Don't try to keep up with the Joneses. You are on the outside looking in. You don't know what goes on behind closed doors. The grass may look greener, but they may be robbing Peter to pay Paul to keep that image.

Analyze TV commercials and store advertisements. Take note of the fads and trends, and don't be so quick to jump on the bandwagon. Don't go into debt to have the latest model car or phone. Also, don't fall victim to get-rich-quick schemes because you are ready to give up your nine-to-five. You don't want to give someone all your money that you could have invested in your own business. I know you want to do what is best for your family, but you need to be careful and smart about what is going on around you.

CHECKPOINT #6: SAY NO

Learn to say no to lower your stress level. It may be a little uncomfortable at first, but it will get easier. Why take on extra tasks or create more debt when you are already loaded with things to do or in a financial bind? I promise, you will feel so much better if you can avoid the extra stress. The person on the receiving end of your "no" will live.

CHECKPOINT #7: CREATE YOUR OWN DEFINITION OF SUCCESS

Don't try to base your success on anyone else. You are where you are because of your decisions and actions. They are where they are because of theirs. If you don't like where you are in life, the power lies within you to change it.

Don't let your perception of success be swayed by the amount of material things that others possess. There are some individuals who have more money than you can imagine, and they are miserable. Would you consider that person successful? Maybe at business, but what about life in general? Is success about money, power, respect, happiness, or having lots of stuff? Take a good look within yourself and figure out what success really means to you.

CHECKPOINT #8: LOOSE LIPS SINK SHIPS

You can't share everything with everybody—not just yet. Not everyone is going to be supportive of you. Don't be surprised when the friends and family members you thought would be supportive aren't. They may seem supportive at first when you are talking about doing things, but when you take action, they switch up on you. They may start to ask why you are doing something because it doesn't make sense to them. But it doesn't have to make sense to them, as long as you have a clear vision on what you are trying to do.

You can't let anyone stop your hustle by creating doubt in your mind. The way you should respond to someone who asks you why you are doing something is to ask them, "Why aren't you?" Don't worry: there will be a time to share with everyone, but the time is just not now. Stick to sharing with your support team only.

CHAPTER 6

GETTING IN THE DRIVER'S SEAT

*You can't use up creativity. The more you use,
the more you will have.*
—Maya Angelou

Getting in the driver's seat may possibly be the most difficult task for some of us. Think back to the time when you got your driver's license. How scary was it when you got in that seat? Although you were nervous, you knew you had to change your mind-set to be a safe driver by learning the rules and preparing to get to your destinations. Each time you got in that seat, it became a lot easier.

You learned the necessary techniques to maneuver through different traffic conditions. You learned how to use your judgment and not to get distracted while driving. Point being, if you never got in that seat, you could never get yourself to your destination. You would put limits on your movement by letting someone else get you where you needed to go on their time.

The same concept applies to being your own boss. The time has come for you to get in the driver's seat. It's time to create your career and financial action plans to attack your list of dreams. It's time to put strategy 3 in play and do some planning.

Use the information from strategy 1 (brainstorming), and strategy 2 (researching)—as well as the rules for being a boss and the mind-set makeover checkpoints I've shared with you—to create separate career and financial plans. Yes, we'll be making two sets of plans, to avoid confusion and keep you from overwhelming yourself. If you feel overwhelmed, you are less likely to continue and more likely to give up.

I can't let you get this far in and give up. So these plans will run parallel to each other. While working directly to get one goal accomplished in your career plan, you should indirectly get a goal accomplished in your financial plan, and vice versa. It might not make sense to you right now, but you will see shortly.

SO HOW DO I GET THERE?

At this point, you should know without a doubt what it is you want to do. Each exercise you have completed has caused a shift in your mind-set. Now you need to set goals to get to those dreams.

Let's take your list of career dreams and determine which are short-term and which are long-term. I strongly recommend that you get a planner that has the full-month calendar pages, weekly agenda, pages for notes, and a calendar for the next year for future planning. Or you can just continue to write in your notebook and put the dates on a calendar.

Your short-term goals are ones that can be obtained within a year. Anything over a year would be considered long-term. This will be very helpful as you create your action plan, ensuring that you are effectively allocating your time and resources to the tasks that should take priority over others. I have three important tips for you to refine your list of goals as you create your career and financial plans:

1. **Be realistic.** Do not set goals that are so far from reality that you will never accomplish them. The key here is to be very honest with yourself and to follow what you want for yourself not others.
2. **Be specific.** Don't be vague in setting your goals, or you won't accomplish anything. Don't just say you want to start a business, or you will never start one. You must state exactly what you want to do.
3. **Set a time frame.** This helps you manage your time to stay focused and on-task, and to avoid procrastinating or rushing to get things done. Being specific in setting a time frame will increase your chances of success, especially if you have a full-time job and a family. Your target dates should be realistic, but not too far out that you still don't get anything accomplished. On the other hand, your target dates should not be so short that you're rushing to get everything done. It's okay to walk; you don't have to run to get to where you want to be. Sometimes slow and steady wins the race.

What do you need to do first to start that business or that dream career? Make a list of those things in the notes section of your planner. Write a specific date for each step to determine short-term and long-term goals. List the short-term goals on your calendar. The long-term goals will remain in your planner in the notes section for future planning for the following year.

With your short-term goals, I don't care if all you need to do is make a phone call, write it down on the day you plan to do it. If there is a course or certification you need to get, do your research, find out where and when it's offered, and put it on your calendar. Of course, if you find out the class starts tomorrow, this is not a realistic time frame. Consider a future date instead.

Do you have paperwork that needs to be completed? Write down in your planner exactly what you need to do and when you think you will be able to complete and submit it. Whatever you need to do, write it down and estimate a date.

WHAT'S YOUR PLAN?

Let's recap:
- Commitment to be your own boss ✔
- List of dreams ✔
- Research on your dreams to know what you really want to do and how to do it ✔
- Short-term and long-term goals in your planner ✔
- Learning the steps to take to create a business ✔

So now you are probably wondering: when do you create your career plan?

Surprise! You've already completed the first part of your two-part career plan. Your planner is your plan! Everything you just put in your planner is an organized month-by-month plan with realistic and specific short- and long-term goals. I hate to disappoint you if you were looking to draft some elaborate plan. I told you from the beginning: I am not trying to overwhelm you. I want you to be a boss just as much as you do. However, I don't want you to do anything you wrote down just yet. You are still in the planning stages, and there are a few other things you need to complete before you implement.

But since you had your heart set on writing a plan, let's have a little fun and create a reward plan to reward yourself for all your hard work. Even as adults, we need to be acknowledged for our hard work. The rewards will keep you motivated and make you feel that all your efforts, no matter how small, are important. There is no right or wrong way to give yourself a pat on the back. Be creative; just don't go overboard.

Now that we've got the fun stuff out of the way, let's get to work on your financial plan. Financial planning isn't going to be as easy as career planning. A little bit of work is required, but it's nothing you can't handle if you've made it this far.

GET ON THE MONEY TRAIN

All aboard! We previously discussed how finances were one of four areas in your life you needed to change your mind-set about. Your finances play a major part in helping you achieve your dreams. When it comes to finances, many of us are in denial. We do things and don't think about the consequences.

For instance, when I went to college, I created a large amount of debt with credit cards, cell phone accounts, retail store credit cards—anything that was offered to an unemployed college student, I took it. I didn't know any better. I wasn't worried about how it was going to get paid back. I just wanted my stuff. Nor did I try to understand why a company would give a jobless college student a credit card. Lord, I really wish I knew then what I know now. How many times have you said or heard someone say that?

There is no need to dwell on your past financial missteps. We are moving forward with a plan to remedy them. You won't even have to come up with the goals for your financial plan; I am going to help you do that. All you need to do is answer yes or no to the following questions:

- Are you debt-free? _____
- Are you current on your bills? _____
- Are you responsible with your credit? _____
- Do you have a rainy-day fund? _____

- Do you have a savings account? _____
- Do you have a monthly budget? _____
- Do you have more than one source of income? _____
- If you have children, do you teach them about these topics? _____

Do not answer any of the questions with *maybe*, *possibly*, or *sometimes*. Just put *no* as your answer. Any question you answer *no* to becomes your financial goal.

I want to put this disclaimer out there that this financial section is meant to be a basic plan that anyone can do. It is in no way any type of professional financial planning service. No complex financial planning is going on over here. I am no financial expert. But I am a woman, a wife, a mother, and an entrepreneur with a plan to live life with options. These are things that helped my family and others that I have advised. And I want the same for you.

Let's take a moment to review each question just to see where your mind-set is and to get it where it needs to be before we proceed through this plan.

ARE YOU DEBT-FREE?

Being debt-free can be your way of life. It is rewarding in more ways than you can imagine. It is all about doing something different from others to break out of a poverty mind-set. My definition of a *poverty mind-set* is a state of mind in which you need to have what you want when you want it—no matter what the cost and even when you know you can't afford it—to keep up with others and portray your lifestyle as something it's not.

A poverty mind-set will cause you to be broke. You think you need something new all the time. You frequently trade in cars to get the newest model instead of paying off your current one to have no car payment. You spend your last dollar to have the latest fashion because you saw it on your favorite celebrity. You must have the newest version of whatever cell phone you have, even though your current one works perfectly fine and you only had it for six months. You furnish your whole house with furniture on store credit, creating an enormous monthly payment instead of just doing one room at a time.

Or maybe you're one of these parents buying their children the latest sneakers that come out for each basketball player—that's two or three hundred dollars you know you can't afford. Why buy your two-month-old a pair of Jordans when he can't even walk? Why not buy them stock in a company each year? Why not open a savings or college fund and add money each year until that child graduates high school? Your son or daughter could put those funds toward starting a business, traveling the world, making a down payment on a starter home, or funding a college education. Set your children up early to be debt-free so they can live life with options. Isn't that a much better gift than fancy sneakers?

There's nothing wrong with spending money if you can afford it. But if you put off paying your bills to do it, then there is a problem. Why are we so obsessed with buying stuff that makes other people rich? Why aren't we concerned about creating wealth for ourselves first, and then spending on whatever our hearts desire because we can afford to do so? The Bible says, "Owe no man anything, but to love one another: for he that loveth another hath fulfilled the law" (Romans 13:8 KJV). Make the necessary sacrifices to be debt-free so you can afford all those things and more. Just think how six months or a year of sacrifices could change your life. You could be on the road to being a self-made millionaire with a shift of your mind-set.

Let's break the cycle, because our children are watching. Get out of this poverty mind-set and get different results out of life. If you are currently debt-free or working on it, you are way ahead of the game. It is certainly in your best interest to reduce your debt before making any career changes. How are you going to change careers or start a business if your personal finances are a mess? You can have a great business concept with awesome products or services, but if you can't manage your money, your business will fail. No ifs, ands, or buts about it—you will run yourself out of business.

Make sure your personal finances are in order before you take your leap of faith. Anything can happen in the blink of an eye. Expect the unexpected. The unthinkable will happen when you least expect it, and of course when you aren't prepared for it. That's not negative thinking; it's called being prepared, and it's a major part of your boss mind-set.

ARE YOU CURRENT ON YOUR BILLS?

If you do have debt, are you current on your payments? What about your monthly household bills? I wish we all could answer yes to this question. However, that is not the reality for some. They live paycheck to paycheck, and that is not the way you want to go through life.

Lord knows my family and I have had our share of financial ups and downs. I know the stress of screening phone calls to avoid bill collectors. You fall into the terrible mind-set that you don't have the money right now for that bill, and they will get it when you get it. That is just terrible, but again, it is a reality for some.

It costs more in the long run to have that mind-set. Think about all the late fees you incur. Add to that higher interest rates on borrowing because your credit scores are lowered, and prolonged payment terms because of deferred or missed payments. Whatever reason you have for being behind on your bills—divorce, loss of employment, widowed, lack of budgeting—there is hope. You may think there is no way to recover, but there is.

It's time to have a talk with your spouse or partner—or yourself, if you are single. Your whole household needs to be involved, or this is not going to work. It will only cause a lot of arguments. I know from experience. When we had the talk in my household, it took a minute, but we all got on the same page. Of course, there were a lot of reminders along the way. But the way my vision of becoming a full-time entrepreneur was set up, I needed my entire household to be working toward the same goal. You must do the same. If you are already current with all your bills, you are a step ahead of the game.

ARE YOU RESPONSIBLE WITH YOUR CREDIT?

Despite all your efforts with the use of credit, sometimes things happen that are out of your control. A person with excellent credit can turn into someone with a negative credit record due to job loss, divorce, or loss of the sole breadwinner in the home. On the other hand, that person just might be a frivolous spender. Regardless, we live in a society where most everything is based on the use of credit, and you are scored on it. That score allows you to obtain some items and determines the interest rate for your monthly payments.

Basically, you need to create debt to get a score. If you don't, you won't get a score, which is just as bad as having a low score because companies can't determine your creditworthiness. Seems like we are set up to fail financially by the society we live in. According to some financial experts, America has a debt trap.[4] Lenders want you to be in debt. Research the phrase "debt trap"—trust me, you will find all types of disturbing information about it.

The next time you watch television, take notice of all the credit card, loan, and car dealership commercials trying to entice you to spend. They make it seem like you are saving hundreds or thousands

---

[4] "Debt Trap," BusinessDictionary.com, retrieved June 6, 2017, http://www.businessdictionary.com/definition/Debt-Trap.html.

of dollars. How are you saving if you are spending money? Also, pay attention when you go in a store to shop. They try to get you to apply for a store credit card as you are walking through the store or at the checkout. They try to entice you with 20 percent off your purchase if you apply, even if you don't get approved. So you get 20 percent off your purchase to create more debt for yourself. Let's say your total purchase is fifty dollars, so when you do the math you are only getting ten dollars off your purchase. And because an inquiry was made on your credit, your score goes down a few points.

Yes, I agree that there is a debt trap, and we are enticed into it by our love of stuff and wanting it now. But just because society dangles the carrot in front of you doesn't mean you should take it. You can't blame anyone else for your lack of willpower. You need to hold yourself accountable and be responsible with your credit, and that includes educating yourself on the fine print before you sign on the dotted line.

Now don't get me wrong. You, as the consumer, aren't the only one to blame. There are industries that use predatory and unethical tactics to get consumers loans—convincing consumers that they are looking out for their customers while really, they are only trying to get a sale. This was the cause of the 2007 housing market crash that caused home buyers to go into foreclosure because they could no longer afford their mortgages.

At that time, home buyers were being offered low introductory interest rates that later returned to regular industry interest rates. I still feel even today that some individuals in the automotive industry uses unethical tactics to get some buyers into new cars. I'm just saying, I have witnessed some shady deals. The real problem is that consumers aren't knowledgeable, and the industries aren't in the business of educating consumers.

Credit is not a bad thing when you change your mind-set to be more responsible and smart with it. Companies reward you for using credit and paying your bills on time by increasing your line of credit or using a reward-point program. You can use those points to get cash back or purchase things like airline tickets. A smart thing to do would be to use your credit card to pay your monthly bills and pay off the balance on the payment due date with the money you were going to spend on them anyway. If you charge anything else, you have the option to pay that completely off too or not. I know a couple who does this, and it inspired me. They use their credit card all month and then pay the balance completely off on the payment due date to earn the points. They use the points to travel.

When you are educated on credit, you see beyond the benefits of just racking up points. You can have a great credit score that gets you lower interest rates if you have not created more debt than your income. Pay your bills on time and only use 30 to 40 percent of your available credit balance. In case you didn't know, your credit score is partly determined by the use of your credit amounts. If you have a five thousand dollar limit on your credit card but the balance you are carrying is four thousand, it lowers your score, even if you make your payments on time and thought you were doing everything right. That is why it is important to educate yourself.

Focus on reducing your debt, paying on time, and not creating new credit accounts. If you already have derogatory items on your credit, don't just start paying accounts off. First, find out if you even need to pay them off. If you do, try to get a reduced amount or a payment plan. There may be errors or items on your report that have been there for so long that they can be removed without being paid.

Research the proper steps to dispute and have negative items removed from your report. If that isn't your cup of tea, then consult a professional. There are programs, companies, and banks that can assist you. Just be careful about scams and hidden fees. Make sure you read the company reviews. There are companies that really do have your best interest at heart.

DO YOU HAVE A RAINY-DAY FUND?

Didn't your parents and grandparents always tell you to save for a rainy day? Did you? My grandfather used to tell me and my cousin that all the time. Did I listen? No. Should I have listened? Yes. Your rainy-day fund is the umbrella that protects you when the unexpected happens—like your car air-conditioner needs to be repaired in the middle of a hot summer—without going into your savings, skipping a bill payment, or borrowing money.

Do you have at least $250, $500, or $1,000 set aside for an unexpected event? Truth be told, most people don't have any money set aside specifically for the unexpected. Not having any money set aside is another reason many families fall into the paycheck-to-paycheck cycle. It's hard to catch up when you aren't prepared. If you don't have a rainy-day fund, get right to work on setting one up. Having a little money put aside is better than none.

You may have to get creative to come up with the money for your fund. I found out that one of my banks would deposit fifty dollars in my savings accounts for referring new members to open an account. There is money out there; you just have to find it. Also, I want to mention that if you are behind on your bills, don't try to catch up and then add money to your fund. You will never get ahead. Something else unexpected will certainly happen that will put you further behind. This is another process you will have to go through. Build your fund first, then catch up.

Your rainy-day fund is not for shopping or eating out. I just had to put that out there, because this will be extra money you will have, but you can't touch it. As a matter of fact, just forget about it until you get in trouble and need it to come to your rescue. Put it in a separate savings account or stash it in a piggy bank. It doesn't matter as long as you can get to it when you are in trouble. If you already have an emergency fund, that is awesome. You are another step ahead of the game.

DO YOU HAVE A SAVINGS ACCOUNT?
A rainy-day fund is important, but so is having additional savings. A savings account is for just what it says: to save for something, not to get you wealthy. You can save to purchase items with cash or to pay off your credit card balance if you choose to make purchases on your card. You can save so much more with less debt, but you don't have to be completely out of debt before you start a personal savings account.

I suggest you do both at the same time. You can earn interest on your money while it's sitting in the bank. It won't be a very large amount, but it is something to add to what you already have. Try to find a bank with a higher savings interest rate and no bank fees. There are some banking institutions that reward you for saving a certain amount each month or opening an account with them. Do your research to determine what works best for you.

Another very important type of savings is for your retirement. How are you contributing to your retirement? Do you have a 401K or an IRA? You won't work all your life, so this is very important for your financial security in your golden years. And don't forget, you won't be an employee for much longer, so an alternative to a 401K is an IRA—more specifically, a Roth IRA, which is what I have. A traditional IRA doesn't tax your contributions but taxes your distributions. A Roth IRA does the opposite.

Sounds better to have the traditional over the Roth, right? I disagree. Think about it: your contributions are going to be much smaller than your distributions. If you go with the traditional, you are getting taxed more than with the Roth IRA. In addition, the Roth IRA grows your money with tax-free compounding, and there isn't any minimum or maximum age requirement to contribute. You are not required to take distributions, and within certain provisions, you can use your money. It's the best-kept millionaire-maker secret. When your kids start working during the summer, one of the best things you can do for them is open up a Roth IRA. They can only contribute earned income into it, and with the compounding interest, they will thank you later.

Side note: Don't just let your money sit idle in a savings account. You should also consider investing money in stocks, bonds, mutual funds, real estate, etc. You need to learn how to grow your money actively and passively to build wealth. When you complete this book, I suggest you continue to educate yourself on investing your money by reading one of my favorite books, *Money: Mastering the Game* by Tony Robbins. This book gave me a better understanding and taught me quite a few things, even as someone with a finance degree. For those who are saving and investing consistently each month already, great job!

DO YOU HAVE A MONTHLY BUDGET?

When it comes to business, budgets are extremely important. Generally, businesses create an annual budget to control spending and track actual and projected expenses. They review monthly to ensure all their expenses are accounted for and they are not over budget. If they are over budget, an adjustment must be made to their spending for the next month to avoid being over budget at the end of their fiscal year. In preparing their budgets, businesses take into consideration recurring and annual expenses like rent, insurance, taxes, utilities, and rate increases. They also have savings for unexpected expenses. These are the same things you should do personally.

Create a monthly and annual budget to track your expenses and income. A budget will give you perspective on your financial situation. If you are living paycheck to paycheck, you will understand why. This will be a big eye-opener for those who think they have it all together without using a budget. Budgets are fun; just wait and see how many times you do your happy dance when you find a way to decrease your expenses and increase your savings and income. Now, I know there are some individuals who already do have a budget, which is great. You may find some tips that will help you make your budget even better.

DO YOU HAVE MORE THAN ONE SOURCE OF INCOME?

In addition to saving and investing, having multiple sources of income is the other major way to build wealth. This is especially important when you are getting your business started. Right now, your full-time assignment may be your only source of income. When most people think about having more than one source of income, they immediately think of a part-time job. However, a part-time job should not be a permanent source of income for you. If you have a part-time job, you don't want to make two jobs your focus; that will only distract you from your own business ventures. You will be too tired to work on your own dreams.

By no means am I telling you to go out and get a part-time job if you have already started your business. But if you are still in the planning stages, it could be a temporary way for you to pay down debt, save money for a specific expense, or have a resource to transition from being employed full-time to part-time to full-time entrepreneur. This may not make sense right now, but trust me—it will in a minute.

Don't just think of a part-time job as a source of income but as a tool to help you get to your other sources of income—and eventually the most important income source, your business income. Maybe getting a part-time job never crossed your mind, but it could be an option for you now that you have a different perspective on what to do with it. A part-time job gives you a consistent source of income and the time you need to build your own business. You go from full-time employee to part-time employee to ease you into becoming a full-time entrepreneur. Don't get so stuck in the mind-set that you must have full-time employment. Use the income to pay off some debt or build up your savings. Do not use this money for shopping. Remember: you can buy everything you want later by making the sacrifice now.

Once you start your business, you'll want to think of ways of creating multiple income streams within and in addition to your primary business. The Bible says in Ecclesiastes 11:2 (NIV), "Invest in seven yea eight streams of income for you do not know what evil may come upon the land." I am working on my seven to eight income streams, as you should. This is where the fun begins. Once you get to the point of expanding your business, taking on new ventures will be second nature to you. There won't be anything you aren't willing to try to do for others.

IF YOU HAVE CHILDREN, DO YOU TEACH THEM ABOUT THESE TOPICS?

Our children not only watch and learn from everything that we do, but also from the world around them. As parents, we must take into consideration even the simple things that we think won't have an impact on our kids and teach them to do better than we did. When I think back on all the financial mistakes I made in college, I know that I can't let my children—or any child, for that matter—make the same mistakes. It is our job to teach them at a young age all that we have learned, mistakes and all.

Most parents set their children up for financial failure without even knowing. Do you talk to your children about finances? Debt? Saving money? Starting their own business? What their interests are? If not, you should. You are the best person to talk to your kids about these things. Find out what motivates your children and encourage them to dream.

Teach them that it is okay to fail at something, but they must always try again. Show them how to have faith that just because it *seems* impossible doesn't mean it *is* impossible. Encourage them to get an education—not just to build someone else's dream but to build their own. Show them how to secure financial stability at a young age, and to build wealth and live abundantly so they can give and create opportunities for others.

Reinforce to them that there is so much more to life than what they see in their community or in the media. Encourage them to travel the world to see it and experience it for themselves. It is important to make sure our youth never lose their sense of imagination. As adults, we tend to lose sight of that. It is important that you teach them not to create limits for themselves. Let's start our youth off young with the "I am my own boss" mind-set.

FINANCIAL STRATEGY

I hope you have a new perspective on your finances and the importance of your financial plan. The only way to get ahead financially is to know the ins and outs of your cash flow. It's time to get to work and take a serious look at your money. We will first review the funds you are currently bringing in.

INCOME/REVENUE

List all sources of income (including employment income after taxes and deductions, business income, investment income, child support, etc.). Calculate monthly total and then annual total.

1. Monthly $_____ × 12 = *put total on line 2*
2. Annual $_____

EXPENSES

Here you are going to list what you spend in five categories: household, annual, miscellaneous, other, and savings.

- Calculate household expenses (rent, mortgage, utilities, car payment, phone, groceries, personal items, insurance, gas, etc.).
    1. Monthly $_____ × 12 = *put total on line 2*
    2. Annual $_____
- Calculate annual expenses (property taxes and any other expense you may have on just an annual basis).
    3. Annual $_____ ÷ 12 = *put total on line 3a*
    3a. Monthly $_____

Tip: Divide the annual expense total by 12 to get the monthly amount to put aside each month to pay the total amount on the annual due date.

- Calculate miscellaneous expenses (entertainment, shopping, dining out, tithes, charitable contributions, gym memberships, cable, online subscriptions, etc.).
    4. Monthly $_____ × 12 = *put total on line 5*
    5. Annual $_____
- Calculate other expenses (personal loans, car loans, student loans, credit card, medical, etc.).
    6. Monthly $_____ × 12 = *put total on line 7*
    7. Annual $_____
- Calculate savings (all types of savings and rainy-day fund).
    A. Monthly $_____ × 12 = *put total on line B*
    B. Annual $_____

SO, WHAT'S LEFT ...

Here is the moment of truth. When you take your total income and subtract your total expenses, what you have left is your disposable income. We will see the true story of your finances here.

1. Total monthly revenue $_____ −
2. Total monthly expenses $_____ =
3. Disposable income $_____

Is your number positive or negative? If your number is negative, then there is a serious problem, and we will discuss that in a second. If your number is positive, that's great—but don't set off the fireworks just yet. Your number is positive because you have enough income to cover all your monthly expenses. But what percentage of your income goes toward your expenses? Using too much of your income puts you at risk if something unexpected happens.

Let's do the percentage calculation with your monthly income and expenses and come back to the annual a little later. For example, say your monthly income is $2,080 and your monthly expenses are $1,500 (do not include your savings amount in this calculation).

$$\$2,080 - \$1500 = \$580$$
$$\$1500/\$2080 = 72\%$$

Your expenses are less than your income, but you are spending 72 percent of your income on expenses. That is a lot, and you haven't even factored in your savings, if you have any. You only have $580 of disposable income left that you can put toward savings. What if you have an $800 unexpected expense? This can be a turning point for you.

Do you have a rainy-day fund or some other savings? If so, you are prepared to handle that unexpected expense. If not, you have just turned your positive into a negative. Now, if your disposable income was positive, I want you to use your actual income and expenses to calculate your percentage, just as I did in the example. What is your percentage? What would happen if you were hit with an $800 unexpected expense?

FINANCIAL SEARCH

You can't just calculate numbers; you also need to analyze the information to truly understand the flow of your finances. This is why I had you list all your sources of income and separate your expenses according to the five categories. The categories will make it easier to identify your necessities, areas of excessive spending, and places where you can cut costs in your budget. When you aren't aware of your spending in proportion to your income, you may spend excessively. This is the reason you need a budget.

Have you ever checked your bank account and wondered, *Where in the world did my money go?* If you were tracking your money like you track your social media statuses, you would never have to ask that question. No need to worry; we will concentrate on increasing your income and cutting your expenses to be 40 percent or less of your income. Then you can use your income to create and build a life with options.

Now, back to your monthly income and expenses. If you calculated a negative number as your total, then Houston, we have a serious problem. You need to find out immediately if the problem is because you have too many expenses, not enough income coming in, or both. Let's revisit your expenses to do a search and rescue of your money.

Lines 1 through 3 of your expenses are necessities, and lines 4 through 7 are luxury items. Your necessities are items that fulfill your basic needs, such as shelter, food, and necessary things for your household. Luxury items are pretty much your wants. First, take a closer look at your monthly necessities. Add lines 1 and 3a, and then subtract the total from your total monthly income. Here comes the moment of truth. If the number is positive, then we know you have enough income to cover the basics. When you factor in the luxury expenses and your number becomes negative, you know you are spending too much money on your wants.

On the other hand, if this number is negative when you subtract just your necessity expenses, unfortunately, you just don't have enough income. Because your income isn't enough to cover the basics, you really need to either increase your income, reduce necessity expenses, cut luxury expenses, or do some combination of those things.

That was a simple analysis of your income and expenses, right? Just a little simple math, but hopefully a wake-up call for you. You've completed the search part of your mission to identify and examine the results of your calculations. It's now time to implement the rescue portion. It's kind of hard to fix something if you don't know what's broken. In your analysis, it doesn't matter if you determined you have too many expenses or not enough income; the plan is to work on both anyway. Make the commitment now. Let's begin your financial rescue mission.

FINANCIAL RESCUE

When you first got on this money train, I asked you if you had more than one source of income. Having more than one source of income is vital in building wealth. Right now, you are only in the foundation stages of the transition from full-time employee to full-time entrepreneur. You must increase the cash flow in your household to pay off debt, save, and invest in you and your business ventures. Let's revisit the idea of acquiring a part-time source of income. This is the most obvious way to bring additional money into your household. It doesn't have to be you who obtains part-time employment. It can be your spouse, partner, or children. It can be done by the traditional route of physically going to an establishment or the nontraditional route of working from home.

I know a couple of people who have become Uber drivers and absolutely love it. They enjoy it so much because they earn extra cash and determine how long and when they are available. No set scheduling, no micromanaging, and no driving to an office. These are very outgoing people, and this fits them perfectly.

Having teenagers work part-time frees up money for you, because they will be able to support their wants while you take care of their needs. My children worked part-time jobs every summer from the time they were fifteen years old. This was a big help when it came to our household finances. There are so many possibilities; you just need to find out what works best for you and your family.

While part-time employment can be a great additional source of income, it's not always an option. Some can't work part-time because of their full-time job assignment schedule or family obligations, or because they've already started their business or are pursuing their dream career. Fortunately, there are alternative ways to add to your current household income. Consider selling items you no longer use, either online or by having a yard sale. You get a little spring cleaning done while bringing in extra cash for your savings or to pay off a bill or two.

In addition, you can sell items you make payments on with an outstanding balance not due within the next twelve to eighteen months. For example, sell your car if you have thirty-six months left to pay off the loan. Use a portion of the money to pay off the loan balance and the rest to buy a cash car, build up your savings, or pay off another bill. This is a great way to get rid of a huge luxury expense. In addition, you can find websites that pay you to be a secret shopper, test products, take surveys, watch videos, browse the Internet, or play games.

If that doesn't work for you then consider becoming an independent consultant for a company selling their products through a website. You won't have to deal with any inventory and you control you schedule. Or offer your services as a freelancer through one of the online sites like Fiverr and freelancer.com. These two options put you completely in control of how much you work and earn.

Maybe none of the previous suggestions work for you. Another alternative would be to consider finding a new full-time job assignment that pays you more than your current job. However, I would only use this as a last resort. It is important to make this type of employment change early. Once you start working on your business, there is no time for you to still be looking for jobs. Remember, you are making these necessary changes early on to improve your financial situation to allow you to quit sooner and be your own boss. Shortly, we will discuss just how much income you need to do that. This is a very important section for those who are looking to quit their jobs to be a boss in their own business.

EXPENSES RESCUE

Now, let's see how you can reduce your expenses. We are going to begin with the necessities. Are there expenses here that you can reduce? Of course. Think about rent, mortgage, car insurance, car payment, groceries, etc. Can you find a cheaper place to live? You may need to downsize or move to a cheaper neighborhood. Focus on necessities, not wants right now.

Here's a tip for homebuyers I learned as a real estate broker. Make an extra payment to your mortgage annually to pay off your home sooner. This decreases the interest owed and knocks years off your mortgage. All you need to do is get your lender to switch your payments to biweekly instead of monthly. You will still have the same monthly amount; you are just splitting the payment from one lump sum into smaller biweekly payments, which results in an automatic extra payment each year.

Consider switching car insurance companies. Nowadays, companies are so competitive for your business they offer all types of discounts. Shop around and get educated on what works best for you and your family situation. We discussed earlier selling your vehicle if the loan balance cannot be paid off within twelve to eighteen months. When you quit your job, you want to avoid large expenses. By doing these things, you will get rid of some huge expenses.

Feeding your family can be an enormous expense depending on the size and how much you dine out. The simple solution is to cook at home more. When you go grocery shopping, make a list of your planned meals based on weekly sales and coupons available. You don't have to do extreme couponing to save on your grocery bill. I didn't have the time, nor did I know all the tricks to extreme couponing. The little I did do reduced my grocery bill for a family of four.

When you cook at home, you have leftovers, snacks, and drinks to take to work or school for lunch, so again you are saving money. Stay away from the vending machines at your job; they are very expensive for something that you can buy a whole pack of from the grocery store. Limit the number of times you eat out, and when you do eat out, use coupons. You can find these in newspapers, online, in the mail, or in fundraiser coupon books. Many are "buy one meal, get one free." Find a lunch buddy on your job to split the cost of the one meal if you don't bring your lunch. You'll get your meal for half the price by splitting the cost of a BOGO.

Also, check your restaurant receipts. They sometimes have surveys you can take to get something free. Challenge yourself to only spend a certain amount per week or to not eat out at all. I did this with one of my friends at work, and it really kept both of us motivated to bring our breakfast and lunch. When we didn't, we used coupons or split a meal. We set our weekly amount for ten dollars, and surprisingly, our goal ended up being not to eat out at all at work.

When you dine out with your family, it is an excellent idea to use coupons as well. The BOGO coupons are very beneficial to couples. My husband and I use them all the time when it is just us without the kids. When we dine in a restaurant, we drink water, or one gets a drink and we share because the other still got water. I know what you're thinking: water? Yes, water, because it's free.

These are just a few tips to save on the necessities. I'm sure once you start, you can get very creative in this area.

Now let's explore your luxury expenses. These are your wants, not your needs. Here is where you will be making the most sacrifices. Do you have a gym membership? How often do you use it? Get rid of it. It is a waste of money if you aren't using consistently. Even if you only pay $10 a month, that adds up to $120 a year. Find a video and do your workouts at home.

Cable or satellite TV can get expensive. You have to pay for a lot of channels you don't even watch just to get the few that you do. Disconnect your cable or satellite TV services and keep your Internet service. Subscribe to an online service to watch TV shows and movies. All you need is the Internet. There are some great services that can save you a ton of money.

Are you a coffee drinker? Do you have to make a daily run to a local coffee shop? Why can't you make your coffee before you leave the house or at work?

What about your shopping habits? Do you buy expensive clothing and shoes? Do you buy things on sale or when you first see them in the store? Do you buy your children expensive clothing, shoes, and electronics, or give them money to hang out with their friends all the time? When you have young kids, you don't have to buy them expensive clothing; they are going to outgrow it just as fast as you buy it. Also, does a three-year-old really need an iPad or an iPhone?

Parents of teenagers, it's time to teach them their first financial lesson and help them to get a job. Then they'll have their own money to buy the things they want while you buy what they need. When my kids were younger, they thought you could just drive up to a little box, stick a card in it, and it would spit money out. I had to educate them that the little box was an ATM, and you had to have money in your bank account to get money out.

My oldest son at a young age told me that *mom* meant "Made of Money." I had a very hard time keeping a straight face. But kids only know what they see. As I began to change my mind-set about my finances, I started having conversations with my kids to change theirs.

Start at a young age educating your children on financial literacy and creating wealth. If your kids are old enough to work, that will cut some expenses. You can even have them pay their cell phone bill or a portion of the car insurance if they have their license. Kids can handle more than we give them credit for. There will come a day when you know all your efforts with your kids have paid off when you see them practicing what you taught them.

These are opportunities for you to make sacrifices now to achieve your financial goals. We are going to create a budget for you to save money and stay on track. First, though, let's explore the topic of savings.

SAVINGS

Your rainy-day fund is the first type of savings you should establish. It is important to prepare for unexpected life events—just like you do with car, life, dental, medical, and business insurance. Your parents or grandparents probably told you to put something aside. But did you listen? I didn't. It puzzles me that our grandparents and great grandparents used to do these things that we are now having to reprogram our mind-sets to get back into. You need to start building your rainy-day fund ASAP. Start off small to build up to $250, then at least $500, next try $750, and finally $1,000.

As I stated before, if you need to catch up on any bills, wait until you have established savings of at least $500. When you get caught up, then you can focus on getting to $1,000. Call your bill collectors to work out a payment plan or get an extension to schedule a future payment so they won't be hounding you. They will be more receptive to you setting up a payment arrangement than just ignoring them.

When you start to eliminate some luxury expenses, you'll get to that $500 quicker. Just imagine the $180 a month you've been paying for cable going into your savings instead. What if you were spending $150 a month eating out for lunch at work, not including the $50 you spend on coffee and breakfast? There's $380 of your $500. If you shop all the time, cut it out, and I am sure you will find the rest of your rainy-day fund.

If you have small children, you can create fun money-savings games for them. One thing that I did with my kids is, we took a large juice bottle and I made a recycle label to stick on it so we could all save our change. We neglect the savings power of a little pocket change. Believe it or not, it adds up fast.

When grocery shopping with small kids, use your coupons. Tell them they are on a scavenger hunt. This will somewhat distract them so they aren't trying to stick other stuff in the cart. Make sure you have something they love that you can reward them with at the end of the shopping trip. They will look forward to doing this each shopping trip, and it keeps you motivated to use your coupons. Come up with your own creative ways to get your rainy-day account set up and funded.

In addition to your rainy-day fund savings account, you will need a separate savings account. We are going to call this your "I quit my job" savings account. This is where you put all the money to sustain your household when you quit. You should be jumping for joy to contribute to this savings account. For singles, I recommend saving at least twelve months of household expenses—mainly because it usually takes about a year of business operation to really start seeing a profit. Typically, during your start-up phase, you are starting from scratch with not much left over to pay yourself. But it doesn't have to take you a year to save for it.

On the flip side, if you are a two-income household, I would recommend that you try to save somewhere between six to eight months of household expenses. Stop frowning. I know this seems like a lot, but remember, we are only talking about your household expenses, which are the necessities.

Let's revisit your income and expense calculations to make some adjustments. Add in any additional income to your revenue section to get a new monthly amount and adjust how much you are putting in savings now. Only include things you will be doing on a consistent basis, not profits from the occasional yard sale. That money would have already been used to pay off a bill or a one-time deposit to one of your savings accounts.

Update your annual totals. Then recalculate your monthly household and luxury expenses, deducting any eliminated expenses. Replace any reduced expenses with the new amount. Update your annual expense totals as well. This time, when you subtract your expenses from your income, you should get a positive number instead of a negative number. Your reduced spending decreases your percentage of income spent on expenses and increases your percentage of income put toward savings. You now have the exact amount you need to put in your savings for your expenses, whether you are a one- or two-income household.

The last thing for you to do is to subtract the amount of income from your employment. If you are planning to ease the transition with part-time employment, leave that in until you make the full transition. You can recalculate to remove that as a source of income when you are ready.

Now you know the exact amount of income you will be losing when you quit your job. To see that number drastically drop may seem a little scary. Don't worry. Now you know how much you need to bring in from your business and other income streams to replace that source of income. You must ensure your business is successfully operating to cover business and personal expenses. I know you will learn to adjust.

During this time of transition, you should save specifically for large-ticket items. If you don't, you can delay your efforts in getting away from your full-time employment. Do you think you were prepared to quit before? Probably not. Are you now equipped with the necessary financial information to prepare yourself to quit? Absolutely!

IT'S BUDGET TIME

You went through your income and expenses with a fine-toothed comb. Perhaps it was a little painful, but you survived. Now you will learn how to maintain all your hard work getting your finances straight. A budget is a tool for you to be proactive with your income instead of reactive to your expenses.

We will use your budget to keep you in the know on each expense, to allocate the correct percentage of your income to specific expenses, and to hold you accountable. Your budget should consist of household monthly expenses along with the due dates and the monthly portion of any annual expenses you are putting aside until payment is due in full. I really recommend you have a separate account to hold money you are putting aside each month for an annual expense like taxes, so you don't mistakenly think you have more money and spend it.

Make sure you can pay bills with your prior week's paycheck, not the week of. This allows for an extra pay week if something unexpected comes up before you've established your rainy-day fund. You are still paying on time and avoiding late fees. If you are having a hard time doing this, I suggest you contact some of the vendors to see if they can change your payment date or if a monthly payment can be split into a biweekly payment.

In creating your budget, you need to first decide how you are going to track. You can go about this the old-fashioned way with pen and paper, create a spreadsheet if you are computer savvy to calculate your totals and percentages, download a budget template, or use an app or software that links to your bank account to track your spending for you. It won't take you long to decide which method works best. I used Excel spreadsheets when I created my family budget. I was savvy in Excel. I used it every day in some of my previous accounting positions.

Next, determine your method of paying your expenses. Are you going to pay everything with cash, checks, or your bank card? Some people are better handling actual cash. If you are, try labeling envelopes for each expense or using an accordion file folder sectioned for each expense to put the cash into. Take the money out of your account and allocate it accordingly for things like groceries, rent, and utilities. If your payment can't be made in cash, use your debit card, since it adds a pending payment to deduct money out immediately. If debit is not a payment option, use a money order or a check as a last resort. Be sure to monitor your account to see how long creditors take to deposit your checks. You do not want to incur any overdraft fees because you forgot about a check that was sitting out there.

On the other hand, you may want to avoid actual cash and prefer to schedule auto payments, checks, or debit cards. Use whichever method is easy for you to track. I used a combination of the two methods to pay bills and monitor our spending. Before, my household would often overspend because I never carried cash. I only used my debit card, credit card, and checks. Even though I checked the bank account often, I still would end up with too many swipes. I wasn't using a budget, so something always went unaccounted for. It was just way too much to remember without having a budget.

Once my household got on track financially, the budget proved to be a lifesaver. It was very helpful to schedule payments for certain bills and pay the rest with cash. I eventually started letting all the bills hit our credit card so we could get the reward points, and I paid those bills off each month. This also helped strengthen our personal credit. There was only one bill that was paid by a check.

My household seemed to be more conscious of our spending when we had money in hand. I really had to plan and stick to our budget. Just figure out what works best for your household. Anything left over goes to savings or to invest, not a new pair of jeans.

All you need to do now is use the strategies we've discussed to stick to your budget. Keep telling yourself that these few sacrifices right now are going to provide you with a lifetime of happiness. Now would be a great time to reward yourself if you haven't already.

But before you do your happy dance, I have one more tip for you during this transition: do not lend money to or borrow money from friends or family. Lending money only puts stress and strain on your finances and relationships if the money cannot be paid back in a timely manner or paid back at all. You will soon be in a position from which you will be able to give money as a gift and create opportunities for others to get out of their poverty mind-set. But that time is not now, and I am sure your friends and family will understand. If not, then that is one of those one-sided relationships I warned you about.

Do not borrow from friends or family for the same reason. Yes, it may be a bit of a struggle, but you can make it work. Think about it: if you can't pay for something, it's because you never had the money to pay for it. If you borrow the money, you are just transferring ownership of your debt. Now you owe your friend or family member instead of your bill collector. Until you change your actions, you will always and forever be in debt.

It's time to get off this money train. I hope this long ride has been prosperous for you. We will now proceed to your employee exit and entrepreneur entry strategy.

CHAPTER 7

READY, SET, GO!

I am no longer accepting the things I cannot change. I am changing the things I cannot accept.
—*Dr. Angela Davis*

The time and moment you have been waiting for has come—the reason you are reading this book and have been putting in the work to transform to the "I am my own boss" mind-set. It's time to move on to strategy 4 and start implementing all those things you've brainstormed, researched, and planned so you can say goodbye to being a full-time employee and hello to being a full-time entrepreneur.

I have created eight simple steps to transition you from full-time employee to full-time entrepreneur. We are going to call this your exit strategy. Look at it this way: if you happen to be in a fire, you follow an exit strategy to safety. Anytime there is a crisis, there is always a way to evacuate. That's the exit strategy. Now let's get to your exit strategy. Here are your eight steps:

1. Write down your vision.
2. Write down the goals for your vision.

3. Make a commitment to fully accomplish your goals and quit your job.
4. Evaluate your finances.
5. Set an "I quit" date
6. Write your employer an "I quit" letter and draft your resignation letter.
7. Take your leap of faith.
8. Take a leap of faith again and quit!

I formulated this eight-step exit strategy to help you evacuate from your career crisis.

I know you are probably thinking, *Eight more things to do!* Well, the good news is, you are already halfway through these steps. You have been doing the work all along to complete Steps 1 through 4. If I had given you this whole list of steps at the beginning of the book, you would have skipped around trying to get through it faster. The key to your success is not to just get through a list of items one at a time. As mentioned earlier, one area overlaps another area while creating a shift in your mind-set. You have been implementing change this whole time. Let's do a quick review of the first four steps:

1. Write down your vision. ✔

    You brainstormed and wrote down exactly what it is you want to do to be your own boss.

2. Write down the goals for your vision. ✔

    You did your research and listed the things you need to do to accomplish your goals.

3. Make a commitment to fully accomplish your goals and quit your job. ✔

    You wrote down your commit date and have been working on changing your mind-set since the day you decided to read this book.

4. Evaluate your finances. ✔

    You went through your finances and planned ways to either increase your income, reduce your expenses, or both. You also found out exactly how much income you will need and what your expenses will be when you quit your job.

Now that you know you've completed half the steps, you should have a tremendous feeling of accomplishment and a burning desire to keep going. It only gets better. The next two steps allow you to have a little fun getting your frustrations out about your current employer.

SET AN "I QUIT" DATE

If you're serious about quitting your job, you should be able to set a date to resign. Changing your mind-set about your career caused you to let go of all the things you were programmed to believe about having a job. Evaluating your finances will help you narrow down when you are ready for this step. Most likely, your finances were the main thing stopping you from being able to leave your full-time assignment.

Let's write this date down and make it a part of your vision. Write it down where you can see it every day. Once you take your leap of faith, you are going to do everything it takes to get out of there by that date. However, you want to be realistic in setting your "I quit" date, as with any other goal.

Write down this date and put it somewhere you will see it every day, especially at your place of employment. It will make you smile every time you see it. When things start going a little left, just look at that date and know it will all be over soon. And if others see that date and asks you what it is, just tell them it's a future appointment you have and smile. No need to elaborate; it's none of their business.

Well, what are you waiting for? Set your "I quit" date!

WRITE YOUR EMPLOYER AN "I QUIT" LETTER AND DRAFT YOUR RESIGNATION LETTER

This step should be the easiest thing you've done since you started reading this book—not to mention the most fun. This is your opportunity to be honest in telling your soon-to-be-former employer and coworkers how you really feel about them, and why you are leaving. Get *everything* off your chest. I don't know anyone who has been completely honest about why they are leaving when they give their notice, including myself. Most of the time, we just give a generic politically correct reason why we are leaving. We have been programmed not to burn any bridges, because you never know who you might need.

Some bridges, however, need to be burned and never ever crossed again. If you want to be an entrepreneur, then be an entrepreneur. Don't leave the door open to cross back over to just being an employee if that isn't your dream. If you are leaving any job, why would you want to cross that bridge again? All the reasons you are leaving should be the same reasons you will never return. Writing this letter is a way for you to get out all your frustrations and political correctness, let go, and burn that bridge.

Now, this letter is not meant to be given to anyone. As a matter of fact, don't let this leave your home. You don't want it to get into the wrong hands. That will be a sure way to get you an involuntary termination date instead of your voluntary "I quit" date.

The second part of this step is for you to draft your actual resignation letter. Type it up and make it official with your "I quit" date. Keep it short and simple. No need to include the lies people normally include, like, "I will miss everyone, and I will keep in touch" or "I have really enjoyed my time here—thank you for the opportunity." Just include how much of a notice you are giving and when your last day will be. (Unless you really mean all that mushy stuff; then you can include it.)

I learned in business school that your employees are your greatest asset, so if your employer felt like you were and treated you as such, you wouldn't be so stressed out about it. My former employers brought out what I needed in me to follow my own dream to run my own company, and they showed me how not to treat people. Anytime you work somewhere and constantly think *that is not how you should treat people*, take it as a lesson learned to be the best you can be when you are the employer.

Go ahead and type that letter up so you can have it ready to submit when your "I quit" date rolls around. Do not allow anyone to see it before that date. Do I need to remind you that you don't want your resignation letter getting into the wrong hands?

TAKE YOUR LEAP OF FAITH

That's right: now I want you to dive into your career plan. It's time to go to work on everything you listed in your planner. The time is now. The longer you wait, the more you will keep finding any excuse to talk yourself out of starting. Once you start, it's not as bad as you thought it would be. You will get some bumps and bruises along the way, but being an entrepreneur is all about taking risks. You must learn how to persevere and be creative in your comebacks when you hit a bump in the road.

Although we make plans, rarely does everything go as planned. Just don't give up on your dreams. If you need to take a break, do so, but don't give up. You have prepared yourself for this very moment by overcoming your fears, shifting your mind-set, and tackling your finances. So, ready, set, go! You will be at the top in your dream career or have your business up and running in no time.

Now is the time to share your accomplishments and plans with everyone. Seeing is believing on both sides of the fence. Some of your friends and family would not have believed you could get done what you did until they saw it. No offense toward you; that just may be the type of person they are. But now that they see it, they will more than likely become your biggest supporters. At this point, any negativity should be a motivator. If your friends and family still can't show you any support after all your hard work and accomplishments, you may want to reevaluate those relationships.

Some of you may have already taken a leap of faith before you even picked up this book; if so, I am excited that you stepped out in faith to follow your dreams. Others of you are just now taking the leap. Either way, you haven't reached your ultimate destination, so pay very close attention to step 8. There is one last crossroad. You must find the right path to transition from your current full-time employment into your dream career or to full-time entrepreneurship. I have been at that same crossroad. While you have already taken the leap of faith once, are you prepared to take the leap twice to literally be your own boss?

Before you complete step 8 of the exit strategy, you must read the next chapter. What are you waiting for?

III

SUNNY DAYS

Strategy 5: Evaluating
Strategy 6: Living

CHAPTER 8

ROUTE CHECK

If you are always trying to be normal, you will never know how amazing you can be.
—*Maya Angelou*

Are you on the right path now? Let's see what's been working and what's not using Strategy 5: Evaluating. If after evaluating what you've done so far you feel that you are making progress, continue working. If you are still running into bumps in the road, don't get discouraged. Take a break, do a little more research to see why things aren't working, and revise your plans.

Maybe you aren't doing too well in a course you need to get to that dream career. Don't give up! Remember, failure is an option. You always have options, whether you think you do or not. If you think you can, you will. If you think you can't, you won't. Right? It's all about your mind-set. Get a tutor if it's not too late. If it is, then repeat the class—except this time, put in the extra study time, meet with the instructor, or get help from your classmates.

Don't be hard on yourself if you need to revise your plans. Focus your time and energy on your comeback. So what if it takes you a little longer than planned? This is not a race, and you aren't in competition with anyone. This is your journey to take by yourself. What's important is that you get all the way through to the finish, not how fast you get there. Stick to your plan, revise as necessary, and stay motivated. Use the same things that motivated you in the beginning to keep you moving forward now.

Success is no accident. It is hard work, perseverance, learning, studying, sacrifice, and most of all love of what you are doing.
— Pele

QUESTIONS FOR EVALUATING YOUR PROGRESS

To effectively evaluate your mind-set shift and strategic-plan progress, there are questions you will need to ask yourself.

QUESTION 1: IS MY PLAN CLEAR, AND HAVE I COVERED ALL FINANCIAL AND CAREER GOALS?

If your plan isn't clear, you aren't going to make any progress. You can't get where you want to go if you don't know how to get there. You're wasting entirely too much time and energy. Time is one thing you can't ever get back, so use it wisely.

You might figure out that you don't want to continue working on one of your career dreams and prefer to move on to something else. There's nothing wrong with that. There's a big difference between wanting to do something but not knowing how to get it done and not wanting to do it at all. Make sure you cover all your bases when it comes to career and finances. You don't want to skip completing a task that is vital to your success, like working on your finances.

QUESTION 2: ARE MY TIMELINES REALISTIC TO COMPLETE MY TASKS?

This is not a race between you and anyone else. You must allow yourself time to effectively complete all the tasks and follow all the tips outlined in this book in order to reach your goals in the most efficient way possible. Don't rush, but don't procrastinate either.

Adjust your deadlines accordingly. If you are making tremendous progress, move up a few deadlines. That should be confirmation that you are on the right path. If you are taking a little longer than planned, try to figure out why. Is it because the process is really going to take that long, or were you just being unrealistic in how soon you could get it done? What about your "I quit" date? Is that realistic?

QUESTION 3: DO I MAKE THE NECESSARY SACRIFICES TO COMPLETE MY TASKS?

Even if you have set a realistic "I quit" date, you must do the work and make sacrifices to get it done. There will be times when you have to skip social gatherings to work on your business, or stay up until two in the morning after putting in an eight-hour shift. You might skip a shopping trip to work on paying off your debt or growing your "I quit" savings. When you can do these without any hesitation, that is a clear sign you have shifted your mind-set.

I had to reset my "I quit" date three times when I first started on this journey because I was dragging my feet. I was working on my plan, but I wasn't getting to all that needed to be done in a timely manner. I didn't give up, though; I kept going to bring my dreams to reality.

QUESTION 4: DO I GET EXCITED WHEN I WORK ON MY PLANS?

Another obvious sign that your mind-set has shifted is that you get excited anytime you work on anything related to becoming your own boss or obtaining your dream career. You don't see your actions as work. You are ready and willing to do whatever it takes without losing the pep in your step. However, if working on your goal plan is causing you more stress and headache than working at your full-time assignment, then maybe what you have been working on is truly not for you. Revamp your action plan and move on to the next item on your list.

I never lose ... Either I win or I learn.
—*Anonymous*

IS BEING MY OWN BOSS REALLY FOR ME?

Your dreams aren't too big; others think too small.
—*Anonymous*

There is nothing wrong with reevaluating your thoughts. Like I said before—and I will say it repeatedly—being your own boss is about changing your mind-set and making boss moves. Make the choice not to accept dysfunction any longer in your life as a norm. Get rid of the distractions and limited thinking about your relationships, personal life, finances, and career. Break free from the chains that hinder you from walking into your destiny.

You must break that poverty mind-set, break those generational curses, break out from toxic relationships, and break away from that "what if I fail?" spirit. You are not obligated to any of these things. They are all options. Poverty is an option. Generational curses are options. Relationships are options. Failure is an option. Anything that is limiting you from your dreams is an option. You are free to choose to stay down or free yourself.

You already have the power. Just step up and activate it with your faith. The process may not be easy, but it is well worth it at the end. Don't quit—you are almost to your destination!

CHAPTER 9

YOU HAVE ARRIVED AT YOUR DESTINATION

Life is not measured by the number of breaths we take, but by the moments that take our breath away.
—*Maya Angelou*

All right: are you ready now to complete step 8 in your exit strategy: "Take a leap of faith again and *quit*?" You have built your business and your brand as a part-time entrepreneur. Don't you wish you had more time to work on your business? Are you ready to jump completely into that new career? Well, your "I quit" date should be approaching. Are your finances in order? Yes! Is your savings account in order? Yes! Have you incorporated your business to utilize business credit and grown it to have consistent multiple income streams? Yes! Time to give up full-time employment and take up strategy 6: Living.

Let's pause for a minute to think about this. If you want to continue to be a full-time employee, your business is only a hobby—just something you do on the side to make some extra cash. You will continue to have the same workforce frustrations as everyone else and continue to make someone else rich. If you have come this far and you aren't willing to take that leap of faith and quit, then maybe being an entrepreneur is not for you. Or maybe having that dream career is just not that important.

Do you agree? Whether you agree or not, that is the reality of it. Entrepreneurs are innovators and risk-takers. Part of being a risk-taker is having faith to take the necessary steps without knowing what is around every corner. So, what's it going to be? How many days are you away from your "I quit" date? When that day comes, are you going to take that leap of faith again? This is what you signed up for when you started reading this book. Let the countdown to your final days of just being an employee begin.

Time is ticking away. You are down to one month, now two weeks. You can finally deliver that resignation letter you wrote months ago to your soon-to-be-ex-employer. Start removing your personal items to put them in your own business workspace or new office. Your last few days are approaching. Exchange contact information with individuals you want to keep in touch with.

Finally, it's "I quit" day. You take the leap of faith again without any hesitation. The transition is complete, and I never doubted you. Now celebrate!

I QUIT. NOW WHAT?

You did it! You quit! You are a full-time entrepreneur, or you have obtained your dream career. It wasn't easy, but you made it to the light at the end of the tunnel. You have freed yourself and are now living out your dreams, living to change the world, living to be your own boss. No one is the boss of you but *you*. You have written your own definition of what success is for you and your family.

So what now? What do you do the day after you quit? The

answer is to live every day from here on out on purpose, intentionally and unapologetically.

NOW I'M LIVING

Just because you have arrived at your destination doesn't mean you kick back and only focus on yourself. While on this journey, I'm sure you experienced many things you can share to motivate other individuals. You not only have the wisdom now but more time and resources to mentor and create opportunities for others. No longer are you a borrower or a lender. You are a giver to help others with no strings attached. Giving is so rewarding, and the feeling you get is indescribable. Wake up each morning with a purpose to do something that will change the lives of others.

Live life intentionally. You are now in a position as an entrepreneur or a top corporate executive where you can create opportunities for others to make their journey a lot easier. Create jobs and programs to support and mentor the community. Be the employer to them that you desired as an employee. Use your platform to end some of that same workforce stress and frustration that you once felt. Create a corporate culture that individuals desire to be a part of as customers, employees, and business partners. When you are a boss, it's not an option—it's your obligation to educate others to be their own boss. Be intentional in everything you do.

Live life unapologetically. Many times, I feel like we unconsciously ask for permission to live out our dreams or apologize for our success. We feel bad for having to leave a job or a toxic relationship with family and friends behind. Don't sabotage your chance to live your life by waiting on the approval of others or by keeping distractions in your life. Be confident in your faith to continue to lead you on your right path. Continue to pursue your dreams, expand on your business ventures, and travel the world. Create memories with your family and friends from once-in-a-lifetime experiences. And don't neglect to make time for yourself.

Build wealth by not only saving money but also saving to invest. Money never sleeps. Learn how to make it in your sleep. Stop creating debt to go broke; use debt to make money. Invest in real estate. Leave a legacy you can pass down from generation to generation. And most importantly, never apologize for living your life with a purpose and being intentional in doing so.

ONE LAST THING

No matter what your motivation is, I hope you're glad you picked this book to read. My purpose for writing this book was to inspire and empower individuals from all walks of life to change their mind-set and follow their dreams. Even though I may not know you personally, I have shared the same workplace stress, financial challenges, and emotional struggles. I knew the only person who could fix it was the person I saw every day in the mirror. I had to stop pointing fingers, change my mind-set, and implement change in my life. I never want to relive those days. I am now on a path to living the life I chose to live, not one others laid out for me.

Writing this book to share my blueprint with you and to provide you with an option for enhancing your quality of life brings me great joy. I hope that you will pay it forward someday and enhance the lives of others one way or another. I hope that each chapter and each concept propelled you closer to achieving your career and financial goals.

Again, congratulations for shifting to the "I am my own boss" mind-set. I wish you much success, unlimited opportunities, and continued growth as you begin to live the life you always dreamed. I am so excited that I could take this journey with you. The pages of this book will forever connect us. I look forward to reconnecting with you in my next book in the "'I Am My Own Boss' Mind-set" series. Please share with others your journey and how this blueprint got you to your destination.

When I became sick and tired of being sick, I decided not to accept any longer what has always been, but embraced my failures as lessons to win at life. No dream is too big if you let your faith light your path and have a boss mind-set. I will always and forever live my life on purpose, intentionally, and unapologetically. Mind-set is everything.
—Tomica Shanelle Atkinson

BUSINESS LESSONS

BUSINESS LESSON #2: STEPS FOR STARTING A BUSINESS
Here is a simple list of steps for starting your business. Add them to your plan if you are seeking to be an entrepreneur. Remember to do you research and consult with a professional as needed.
1. *Write a detailed business plan.* Create a written guide to your products or services, start-up costs, funding needed, location, and method of delivery (such as storefront or online, type of customers, marketing, projected sales).
2. *Determine your business structure.* Choose from sole proprietorship, partnership, LLC, or corporation. You can read more about these in chapter 4. Check with an attorney for legal advice and an accountant for tax advice.
3. *Determine and register your business name.* Depending on your business structure, you may need to register your name with your local or state government. Check with the local county registrar of deeds or state division of corporation for details.
4. *Register for a tax identification number.* Obtain your business employment identification number (EIN) from the IRS either online, by mail, or by phone.
5. *If applicable, register for state and local sales tax numbers.* Contact your state department of revenue agency for details.

6. *Obtain business licenses and permits.* Verify if any federal, state, or local licenses or permits are required.
7. *Open a business checking and savings account.* Use your EIN to open business accounts separate from your personal. Make sure to open both savings and checking; you can use your business savings as collateral once you build your business credibility to get bank financing if necessary.
8. *Locate local and state resources* to assist you in understanding your business obligations, funding options, industry updates, etc.
9. *Create a website and/or social media accounts.* In this digital age, this is the platform to reach millions of customers to market and sell to. Your customers will have your products and services right at their fingertips.

BUSINESS LESSON #3: ELEMENTS OF A FORMAL BUSINESS PLAN

Your business plan is the owner's manual for your business. It can be used as an internal written guide to document such things as your products or services, customer demographics, marketing strategies, projected cash flow, and organizational chart of employees. It does not need to be formal if you won't be presenting it outside of your company. You will need a formal written business plan to present externally to banks or investors for funding.

Below is an overview of each section. You can always find a good template relatable to your business and use it as a guide; hire a professional to help; or utilize your local small business center or the US Small Business Administration, which is a great resource for us DIYers. Once you complete your business plan, be sure to follow instructions from the bank or investor on how they want you to submit your documents.

TITLE PAGE

Include your business name, address, and contact information, including business phone, website, and e-mail. Also include the date and a confidentiality statement if deemed necessary.

EXECUTIVE SUMMARY

The executive summary clearly states the purpose of your business for the target audience. I have always been advised to write this section last.

COMPANY DESCRIPTION

Describe everything about your business. Include details on what you do, what differentiates you from other businesses in the industry, who your customers are, and where you are located.

MARKET ANALYSIS

It is extremely important to research your industry to know who your customers and competitors are. You may want to describe in detail your existing or potential customers, why you chose that market, the size of your market, and any changes you expect within your target market. List your competitors, their strengths and weaknesses, and your strengths and weaknesses as well.

ORGANIZATION AND MANAGEMENT

Describe in detail the organizational and management structure of your business. Explain who the owners and managers are. Attach a résumé in the appendix if you choose, in addition to explaining these individuals' background and experience as it relates to the business.

SERVICE OR PRODUCTS

Give specific details on your products and services. Include how much they cost, the benefits to your customers, and the life cycle.

MARKETING STRATEGY

Here you will list how you plan to market your business and sell your products or services. Explain how often you will use these strategies.

FUNDING REQUEST

This section is very important if you are seeking funding for your business. Include details of how much you are seeking. Then list exactly what you plan to use it for, such as employees, supplies, equipment, and buildings.

FINANCIAL PROJECTIONS

This section is critical for your funding efforts. Financial projections help convince prospective lenders and investors that your business will be profitable by offering a good return on investment. You must project your cash flow here to prove you will be able to pay back the bank or investor over a certain time frame. This is only an estimate, but you do have to show that you will be able to pay them back.

APPENDIX

The appendix is not a mandatory category to include in your business plan. However, it is useful to include information like résumés, lease agreements, contracts, permits, licenses, or anything that you want the bank or investor to see.

BUSINESS LESSON #4: BUILDING BUSINESS CREDIT

Business credit is linked directly to your business name and EIN, not to your consumer credit and SSN. Your business must meet certain criteria for approvals to eliminate using your consumer credit as a personal guarantee. Here is an overview of the process to show business credibility so you can acquire business credit.

- *Choose your business name wisely.* Some credit issuers and lenders will deny you based on your name. Some industries are restricted or high-risk, so banks won't lend to you if your name suggests you are doing business in one of those industries.
- *Incorporate your business.* This separates you personally from your business. Be sure to use your name on listings, licenses, or bank statements exactly as it is registered.
- *Get your EIN from www.irs.gov.* This is free, so do not pay someone to get it for you. Also register with the state to get your account ID, if applicable.
- *Set up a physical business address if possible.* Don't use a post office box when applying for funding, or you will get denied. If you don't have a storefront, try a virtual office. When using a virtual office, make sure the address is going to show as your business. Use your home address as a last resort.
- *Set up a business phone and fax number.* Your number needs to be listed with 411, and get a 1-800 number as well. Do not use a personal cell or home phone number when applying for credit.
- *Set up a professional business website for your products or services*, with a professional e-mail that has your domain name, not a personal Yahoo, Gmail, or Hotmail e-mail.
- *Open your business checking and savings account.* Be sure to use your name exactly as it is registered.

- *Obtain any licenses and permits for your business* with your name exactly the way it is registered.
- *Register for your free Dun & Bradstreet DUNS number.* Your DUNS number is a nine-digit identifier used to establish business credit with a credit profile. It is like your personal SSN, but it is used only for business.
- *Sign up for business credit reporting and monitoring with D&B, Experian, and Equifax.* Your business credit score is called a Paydex score. Unlike consumer credit, your business credit is exclusively determined by making timely payments. The sooner you pay when you receive your bill, the higher your score will go, along with the more lines and usage of credit you have. A Paydex score between 75 to 100 is where you want to be.
- *Start applying for business credit* in the following order:
    o vendor accounts that are net 30-day terms, at least five payment experiences
    o revolving retail store credit cards
    o revolving cash credit cards that you can use anywhere, or bank financing

www.ingramcontent.com/pod-product-compliance
Lightning Source LLC
Chambersburg PA
CBHW022022170526
45157CB00003B/1315